CLYMER®
MANUALS

BMW
500 & 600cc TWINS • 1955-1969

WHAT'S IN YOUR TOOLBOX?

More information available at haynes.com
Phone: 805-498-6703

**J H Haynes & Co. Ltd.
Haynes North America, Inc.**

ISBN-10: 0-89287-224-1
ISBN-13: 978-0-89287-224-4

M308, 12S1, 14-160

Common spark plug conditions

NORMAL
Symptoms: Brown to grayish-tan color and slight electrode wear. Correct heat range for engine and operating conditions.
Recommendation: When new spark plugs are installed, replace with plugs of the same heat range.

WORN
Symptoms: Rounded electrodes with a small amount of deposits on the firing end. Normal color. Causes hard starting in damp or cold weather and poor fuel economy.
Recommendation: Plugs have been left in the engine too long. Replace with new plugs of the same heat range. Follow the recommended maintenance schedule.

CARBON DEPOSITS
Symptoms: Dry sooty deposits indicate a rich mixture or weak ignition. Causes misfiring, hard starting and hesitation.
Recommendation: Make sure the plug has the correct heat range. Check for a clogged air filter or problem in the fuel system or engine management system. Also check for ignition system problems.

ASH DEPOSITS
Symptoms: Light brown deposits encrusted on the side or center electrodes or both. Derived from oil and/or fuel additives. Excessive amounts may mask the spark, causing misfiring and hesitation during acceleration.
Recommendation: If excessive deposits accumulate over a short time or low mileage, install new valve guide seals to prevent seepage of oil into the combustion chambers. Also try changing gasoline brands.

OIL DEPOSITS
Symptoms: Oily coating caused by poor oil control. Oil is leaking past worn valve guides or piston rings into the combustion chamber. Causes hard starting, misfiring and hesitation.
Recommendation: Correct the mechanical condition with necessary repairs and install new plugs.

GAP BRIDGING
Symptoms: Combustion deposits lodge between the electrodes. Heavy deposits accumulate and bridge the electrode gap. The plug ceases to fire, resulting in a dead cylinder.
Recommendation: Locate the faulty plug and remove the deposits from between the electrodes.

TOO HOT
Symptoms: Blistered, white insulator, eroded electrode and absence of deposits. Results in shortened plug life.
Recommendation: Check for the correct plug heat range, over-advanced ignition timing, lean fuel mixture, intake manifold vacuum leaks, sticking valves and insufficient engine cooling.

PREIGNITION
Symptoms: Melted electrodes. Insulators are white, but may be dirty due to misfiring or flying debris in the combustion chamber. Can lead to engine damage.
Recommendation: Check for the correct plug heat range, over-advanced ignition timing, lean fuel mixture, insufficient engine cooling and lack of lubrication.

HIGH SPEED GLAZING
Symptoms: Insulator has yellowish, glazed appearance. Indicates that combustion chamber temperatures have risen suddenly during hard acceleration. Normal deposits melt to form a conductive coating. Causes misfiring at high speeds.
Recommendation: Install new plugs. Consider using a colder plug if driving habits warrant.

DETONATION
Symptoms: Insulators may be cracked or chipped. Improper gap setting techniques can also result in a fractured insulator tip. Can lead to piston damage.
Recommendation: Make sure the fuel anti-knock values meet engine requirements. Use care when setting the gaps on new plugs. Avoid lugging the engine.

MECHANICAL DAMAGE
Symptoms: May be caused by a foreign object in the combustion chamber or the piston striking an incorrect reach (too long) plug. Causes a dead cylinder and could result in piston damage.
Recommendation: Repair the mechanical damage. Remove the foreign object from the engine and/or install the correct reach plug.

CONTENTS

QUICK REFERENCE DATA

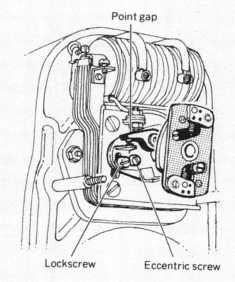

Point gap

CONTACT
BREAKER
ASSEMBLY

Lockscrew   Eccentric screw

TIMING MARKS

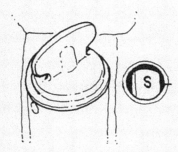

S mark aligned
(Correct static timing)

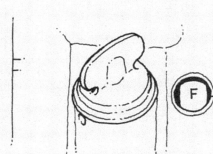

F mark aligned
(Correct advanced timing)

TUNE-UP SPECIFICATIONS

Item	Torque
Head bolt torque	3.3-3.7 mkg (24-27 ft.-lb.)
Valve clearance	
Intake	0.15mm (0.006 in.)
Exhaust	0.20mm (0.008 in.)
Point gap	0.35-0.40mm (0.014-0.016 in.)
Spark plug gap	0.6mm (0.024 in.)
Static timing	9° BTDC (at S mark)
Advance timing	F mark aligns at 5,800 rpm
Idle speed	500-750 rpm

RECOMMENDED SPARK PLUGS

Recommended Plug	
Type	
R50, R60	Bosch W 240 T1, T2 (see **Plug Length**)
R69	Bosch W 240 T1, T2 during break-in
	Bosch W 260 T1, T2 after break-in (see **Plug Length**)
Plug length	R50 up to frame No. 647 000—T1
	R60 up to frame No. 1 817 300—T1
	R69 up to frame No. 654 950—T1
	All subsequent models use long-reach T2 plugs

NOTE: Plug bore in cylinder head is unmarked for short-reach plugs; for long-reach plugs, plug bore is stamped "LK".

CAPACITIES

Item	Capacity
Engine oil	2 quarts, 4 ounces (see **Recommended Oils**)
Transmission	1.7 pints (see **Recommended Oils**)
Drive shaft	100cc SAE 90 hypoid gear oil
Final drive	250cc SAE 90 hypoid gear oil
Front forks	265cc (each leg) for refill; 280cc after disassembly
	• Shell 400 shock absorber oil
	• BP Olex HL 2463
	• Belray 5W shock oil

RECOMMENDED OILS

	Temperature/Season	Viscosity
Engine	75 °F and above	SAE 40
	32 °F to 75 °F	SAE 30
	32 °F and below	SAE 10W-30
Transmission	Summer	SAE 90 hypoid gear oil
	Winter	SAE 80 hypoid gear oil

CHAPTER ONE

GENERAL INFORMATION

BMW opposed twins have a deserved reputation for strong performance and long service life. Their potential can best be realized through careful, periodic maintenance. This handbook covers all service operations—from changing a spark plug to overhauling the engine—in a format intended to be understandable to a home mechanic.

MODELS

This handbook covers R 50, R 50/2, R 50 S, and R 50 US; R 60, R 60/2, and R 60 US; R 69, R 69 S, and R 69 US models.

The models are recognized by their rear spring/shock units mounted to the rear frame at the base of the upper half of the units, rather than at the top as is the case with later models. Front suspension on all but the most recent models of the early series is an Earles-type leading link fork. On the later models designated US, suspension is conventional telescopic fork.

To accurately identify a given motorcycle, examine the serial number and manufacturer's plate (**Figure 1**).

MANUAL ORGANIZATION

The service procedures in this manual are grouped by major subassembly (e.g., engine, transmission, fuel system, etc.) to speed work.

In addition, an easy-to-use troubleshooting guide is provided. Common maintenance tasks and tune-up are covered in a single chapter because they are the most frequently performed tasks.

Dimensions, capacities, and weights are expressed both metrically and in terms familiar to American mechanics. When working with critical dimensions (cylinder-to-piston clearance, crankshaft journal diameters, oil pump rotor clearances, etc.), the metric values should be used to ensure accuracy.

SERVICE HINTS

Most of the service procedures described can be performed by anyone reasonably handy with tools. It is suggested, however, that you carefully consider your own capabilities before attempting any operation which involves major disassembly of the engine or transmission.

Some operations, for example, require the use of a press. It would be wiser to have them performed by a shop equipped for such work, rather than to try to do the job yourself with makeshift equipment. Other procedures require precision measurements, and unless you have the skills and equipment to make them, it would be better to have a motorcycle shop help in the work.

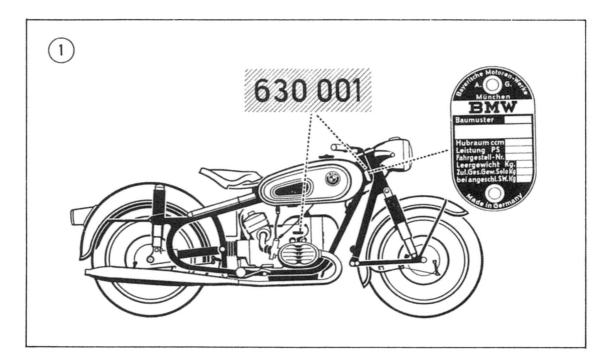

Repairs can be made faster and easier if the motorcycle is clean before you begin work. There are special cleaners for washing the engine and related parts. Just brush or spray on the solution, let it stand, then rinse it away with a garden hose. Clean all oily or greasy parts with cleaning solvent as you remove them.

WARNING
Never use gasoline as a cleaning agent. It presents an extreme fire hazard.

Always work in a well-ventilated area when using cleaning solvent. Keep a fire extinguisher, rated for gasoline fires, handy just in case.

Special tools are required for some service procedures. Some of these may be purchased through BMW dealers. If you are on good terms with the dealer's service department, you may be able to borrow or rent some tools.

Much of the labor charge for repairs made by dealers is for removal and disassembly of other parts to reach the defective one. It is frequently possible to do all of this yourself, then take the affected subassembly to the dealer for repair.

Once you decide to tackle a job yourself, read the entire section in this handbook pertaining to it. Study the illustrations and the text until you have a thorough idea of what's involved. If special tools are required, make arrangements to get them before you begin work. It's frustrating to get part way into a job and then discover that you are unable to complete it.

Collect the necessary tools, parts, lubricants, and cleaning supplies before starting a job. It's to your advantage to have your work area scrupulously clean to reduce the possibility of contamination of precision parts and critical surfaces. You'll also find that a few metal baking pans or sandwich bags and tape are handy for organizing and storing nuts, bolts, washers, and small bits and pieces as they are removed from the motorcycle.

TOOLS

To properly service your motorcycle, you will need an assortment of ordinary hand tools. As a minimum, these include:

1. Combination wrenches (metric)
2. Socket wrenches (metric)
3. Plastic mallet
4. Small hammer
5. Snap ring pliers

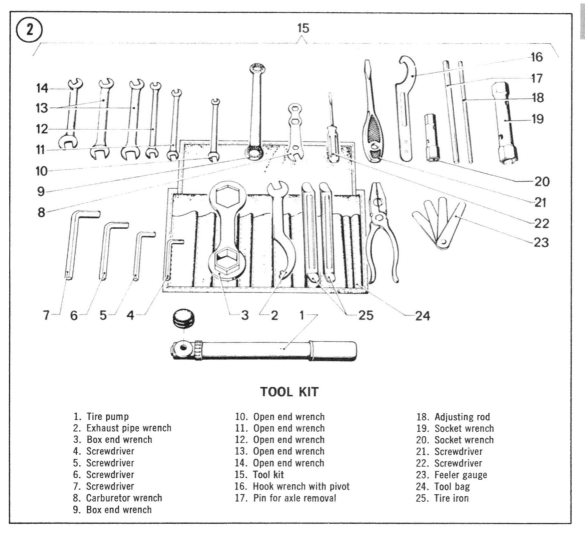

TOOL KIT

1. Tire pump	10. Open end wrench	18. Adjusting rod
2. Exhaust pipe wrench	11. Open end wrench	19. Socket wrench
3. Box end wrench	12. Open end wrench	20. Socket wrench
4. Screwdriver	13. Open end wrench	21. Screwdriver
5. Screwdriver	14. Open end wrench	22. Screwdriver
6. Screwdriver	15. Tool kit	23. Feeler gauge
7. Screwdriver	16. Hook wrench with pivot	24. Tool bag
8. Carburetor wrench	17. Pin for axle removal	25. Tire iron
9. Box end wrench		

6. Phillips screwdrivers

7. Slot screwdrivers

8. Impact driver

9. Allen wrenches (metric)

10. Pliers

11. Feeler gauges

12. Spark plug gauge

13. Spark plug wrench

14. Dial indicator

15. Drift

An original equipment tool kit, like the one shown in **Figure 2**, is available through most BMW dealers and is suitable for minor servicing.

Special tools necessary are shown in the chapters covering the particular repair in which they are used.

Electrical system servicing requires a voltmeter, ohmmeter, or other device for determining continuity, and a hydrometer for battery equipped machines.

Engine tune-up and troubleshooting procedures require a few more tools.

Timing Gauge

By screwing this instrument into the spark plug hole, piston position may be determined. The tool shown in **Figure 3** costs about $20, and is available from larger dealers and mail order houses. Less expensive ones, which utilize a vernier scale instead of a dial indicator, are also available. They are satisfactory, but are not quite so quick and easy to use.

Hydrometer

This instrument (**Figure 4**) measures state of charge of the battery, and tells much about bat-

tery condition. Such an instrument is available at any auto parts store and through most large mail order outlets. A satisfactory one costs less than $3.

Multimeter or VOM

This instrument (**Figure 5**) is invaluable for electrical system troubleshooting and service. A few of its functions may be duplicated by locally fabricated substitutes, but for the serious hobbyist, it is a must. Its uses are described in the applicable sections of this book. Prices start at

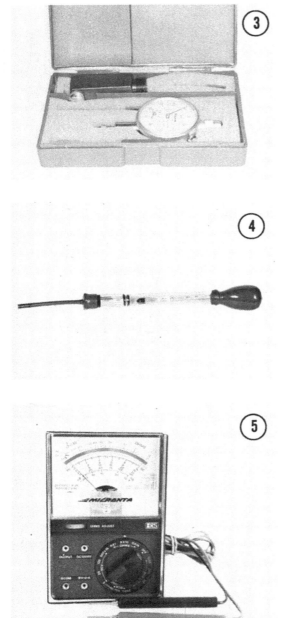

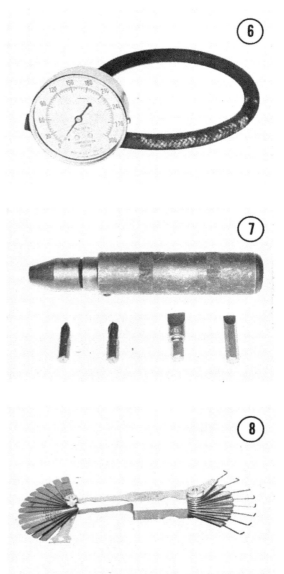

around $10 at electronics hobbyist stores and mail order outlets.

Compression Gauge

An engine with low compression cannot be properly tuned and will not develop full power. A compression gauge (**Figure 6**) measures engine compression. (The one shown has a flexible stem, which enables it to reach cylinders where there is little clearance between the cylinder head and frame.) Inexpensive ones start around $3, available at auto accessory stores or by mail order from large catalog order firms.

Impact Driver

The impact driver (**Figure 7**) might have been designed with the motorcyclist in mind. It makes removal of engine cover screws easy, and eliminates damaged screw slots. Good ones run about $12 at larger hardware stores.

Ignition Gauge

The ignition gauge (**Figure 8**) measures point gap. It also has round wire gauges for measuring spark plug gap.

A few special tools may also be required for major engine service. They are available at BMW dealers.

EXPENDABLE SUPPLIES

Certain expendable supplies are also required. These include grease, oil, gasket cement, wiping rags, cleaning solvent, and distilled water. Ask your dealer for the special locking compounds, silicone lubricants, and commercial cable lube products which make motorcycle

maintenance simpler and easier. Solvent is available at most service stations and distilled water for the battery is available at most supermarkets.

SAFETY HINTS

A professional mechanic can work for years and never sustain a serious injury. If you observe a few rules of common sense and safety, you can enjoy many hours safely servicing your own machine. You can also hurt yourself or damage your motorcycle if you ignore these rules.

1. Never use gasoline as a cleaning solvent.

2. Never smoke or use a torch around flammable liquids, such as cleaning solvent.

3. Never smoke or use a torch in areas where batteries are being charged. Highly explosive hydrogen gas is formed during the charging process. Never arc the terminals of a battery to see if it has a charge; the sparks can ignite the explosive hydrogen as easily as an open flame.

4. If welding or brazing is required on the motorcycle, remove the fuel tank and set it a safe distance away—at least 50 feet.

5. Always use the correct size wrench for turning nuts and bolts, and when a nut is tight, think for a moment what would happen to your hand if the wrench were to slip.

6. Keep your work area clean and uncluttered.

7. Wear safety goggles in all operations involving drilling, grinding, or the use of a chisel or air hose.

8. Do not use worn tools.

9. Keep a fire extinguisher handy. Be sure it is rated for gasoline and electrical fires.

CHAPTER TWO

TROUBLESHOOTING

Diagnosing mechanical problems is relatively simple if you use orderly procedures and keep a few basic principles in mind.

The troubleshooting procedures in this chapter analyze typical symptoms, and show logical methods of isolating causes. These are not the only methods. There may be several ways to solve a problem, but only a systematic, methodical approach can guarantee success.

Never assume anything. Don't overlook the obvious. If you are riding along and the bike suddenly quits, check the easiest, most accessible problem spots first. Is there gasoline in the tank? Is the gas petcock in the ON or RESERVE position? Has a spark plug wire fallen off? Check ignition switch. Sometimes the weight of keys on a key ring may turn the ignition off suddenly.

If nothing obvious turns up in a cursory check, look a little further. Learning to recognize and describe symptoms will make repairs easier for you or a mechanic at the shop. Describe problems accurately and fully. Saying that "it won't run" isn't the same as saying "it quit on the highway at high speed and wouldn't start," or that "it sat in my garage for three months and then wouldn't start."

Gather as many symptoms together as possible to aid in diagnosis. Note whether the engine lost power gradually or all at once, what color smoke (if any) came from the exhaust, and so on. Remember that the more complicated a machine is, the easier it is to troubleshoot because symptoms point to specific problems.

After the symptoms are defined, areas which could cause problems are tested and analyzed. Guessing at the cause of a problem may provide the solution, but it can easily lead to frustration, wasted time, and a series of expensive, unnecessary parts replacements.

You don't need fancy equipment or complicated test gear to determine whether repairs can be attempted at home. A few simple checks could save a large repair bill and time lost while the bike sits in a dealer's service department. On the other hand, be realistic and don't attempt repairs beyond your abilities. Service departments tend to charge heavily for putting together a disassembled engine that may have been abused. Some won't even take on such a job—so use common sense, don't get in over your head.

OPERATING REQUIREMENTS

An engine needs three basics to run properly: correct gas/air mixture, compression, and a spark at the right time. If one or more are missing, the engine won't run. The electrical system is the weakest link of the three basics. More problems result from electrical breakdowns than from any other source. Keep that in mind before you begin tampering with carburector adjustments and the like.

If a bike has been sitting for any length of time and refuses to start, check the battery for a charged condition first, and then look to the gasoline delivery system. This includes the tank, fuel petcocks, lines, and the carburetors. Rust may have formed in the tank, obstructing fuel flow. Gasoline deposits may have gummed up carburetor jets and air passages. Gasoline tends to lose its potency after standing for long periods. Condensation may contaminate it with water. Drain the old gas and try starting with a fresh tankful.

TROUBLESHOOTING INSTRUMENTS

Chapter One lists many of the instruments needed and detailed instructions on their use.

STARTING DIFFICULTIES

Check gas flow first. Remove the gas cap and look into the tank. If gas is present, pull off a fuel line at the carburetor and see if gas flows freely. If none comes out, the fuel tap may be shut off, blocked by rust or foreign matter, or the fuel line may be stopped up or kinked. If the carburetor is getting usable fuel, turn to the electrical system next.

Check that the battery is charged by turning on the lights or by beeping the horn. Refer to your owner's manual for starting procedures with a dead battery. Have the battery recharged if necessary.

Pull off a spark plug cap, remove the spark plug, and reconnect the cap. Lay the plug against the cylinder head so its base makes a good connection, and turn the engine over with the kickstarter. A fat, blue spark should jump across the electrodes. If there is no spark, or only a weak one, there is electrical system trouble. Check for a defective plug by replacing it with a known good one. Don't assume a plug is good just because it's new.

Once the plug has been cleared of guilt, but there's still no spark, start backtracking through the system. If the contact at the end of the spark plug wire can be exposed, it can be held about ⅛ inch from the head while the engine is turned over to check for a spark. Remember to hold the wire only by its insulation to avoid a nasty shock. If the plug wires are dirty, greasy, or wet, wrap a rag around them so you don't get shocked. If you do feel a shock or see sparks along the wire, clean or replace the wire and/or its connections.

If there's no spark at the plug wire, look for loose connections at the coil and battery. If all seems in order there, check next for oily or dirty contact points. Clean points with electrical contact cleaner, or a strip of paper.

No spark at the points with this test indicates a failure in the ignition system. Refer to Chapter Three (*Periodic Maintenance and Tune-up*) for checkout procedures for the entire system and individual components. Refer to the same chapter for checking and setting ignition timing.

Note that spark plugs of the incorrect heat range (too cold) may cause hard starting. Set gaps to specifications. If you have just ridden through a puddle or washed the bike and it won't start, dry off plugs and plug wires. Water may have entered the carburetor and fouled the fuel under these conditions, but wet plugs and wires are the more likely problem.

If a healthy spark occurs at the right time, and there is adequate gas flow to the carburetor, check the carburetor itself at this time. Make sure all jets and air passages are clean, check float level, and adjust if necessary. Shake the float to check for gasoline inside it, and replace or repair as indicated. Check that the carburetors are mounted snugly, and no air is leaking past the manifold. Check for a clogged air filter.

Compression, or the lack of it, usually enters the picture only in the case of older machines. Worn or broken pistons, rings, and cylinder bores could prevent starting. Generally, a gradual power loss and harder starting will be readily apparent in this case.

Compression may be checked in the field by turning the kickstarter by hand and noting that an adequate resistance is felt.

An accurate compression check gives a good idea of the condition of the basic working parts of the engine. To perform this test, you need a compression gauge. The motor should be warm.

1. Remove the plug on the cylinder to be tested and clean out any dirt or grease.

2. Insert the tip of the gauge into the hole, making sure it is seated correctly.

3. Open the throttle all the way and make sure the chokes on the carburetors are open.

4. Crank the engine several times and record the highest pressure reading on the gauge. Run the test on each of the cylinders.

5. The normal compression is 125-147 psi. If the readings are significantly lower than 125 psi as a group, or if they vary more than 15 psi between cylinders, proceed to the next step.

6. Pour a tablespoon of motor oil into the suspect cylinder and record the compression.

If oil raises the compression significantly—10 psi in an old engine—the rings are worn and should be replaced.

If the compression does not rise, one or both valves are probably not seating correctly.

Valve adjustments should be checked next. Sticking, burned, or broken valves may hamper starting. As a last resort, check valve timing.

POOR IDLING

Poor idling may be caused by incorrect carburetor adjustment, incorrect timing, or ignition system defects. Check the gas cap vent for an obstruction.

MISFIRING

Misfiring can be caused by a weak spark or dirty plugs. Check for fuel contamination. Run the machine at night to check for spark leaks along plug wires and under spark plug cap.

WARNING
Do not run engine in dark garage to check for spark leaks. There is considerable danger of carbon monoxide poisoning.

If misfiring occurs only at certain throttle settings, refer to the fuel system chapter for the specific carburetor circuits involved. Misfiring under heavy load, as when climbing hills or accelerating, is usually an indication of bad spark plugs.

FLAT SPOTS

If the engine seems to die momentarily when the throttle is opened and then recovers, check for a dirty main jet in the carburetor, water in the fuel, or an excessively lean mixture.

POWER LOSS

Poor condition of rings, pistons, or cylinders will cause a lack of power and speed. Ignition timing should be checked.

OVERHEATING

If the engine seems to run too hot all the time, be sure you are not idling it for long periods. Air-cooled engines are not designed to operate at a standstill for any length of time. Heavy stop and go traffic is hard on a motorcycle engine. Spark plugs of the wrong heat range can burn pistons. An excessively lean gas mixture may cause overheating. Check ignition timing. Don't ride in too high a gear. Broken or worn rings may permit compression gases to leak past them, heating heads and cylinders excessively. Check oil level and use the proper grade lubricants.

ENGINE NOISES

Experience is needed to diagnose accurately in this area. Noises are hard to differentiate and harder yet to describe. Deep knocking noises usually mean main bearing failure. A slapping noise generally comes from loose pistons. A light knocking noise during acceleration may be a bad connecting rod bearing. Pinging should be corrected immediately or damage to pistons will result. Compression leaks at the head-cylinder joint will sound like a rapid on-and-off squeal.

PISTON SEIZURE

Piston seizure is caused by incorrect piston clearances when fitted, fitting rings with improper end gap, too thin an oil being used, incorrect spark plug heat range, or incorrect ignition timing. Overheating from any cause may result in seizure.

EXCESSIVE VIBRATION

Excessive vibration may be caused by loose motor mounts, worn engine or transmission bearings, loose wheels, worn siwinging arm bushings, a generally poor running engine, broken or cracked frame, or one that has been damaged in a collision. See also *Poor Handling*.

CLUTCH SLIP OR DRAG

Clutch slip may be due to worn plates, improper adjustment, or glazed plates. A dragging clutch could result from damaged or bent plates, improper adjustment, or uneven clutch spring pressure.

All clutch problems, except adjustments or cable replacement, require removal to identify the cause and make repairs.

1. *Slippage*—This condition is most noticeable when accelerating in high gear at relatively low speed. To check slippage, drive at a steady speed in 4th or 5th gear. Without letting up the accelerator, push in the clutch long enough to let engine speed increase (one or two seconds). Then let the clutch out rapidly. If the clutch is good, engine speed will drop quickly or the bike will jump forward. If the clutch is slipping, engine speed will drop slowly and the bike will not jump forward.

Slippage result from insufficient clutch lever free play, worn friction plates, or weak springs. Riding the clutch can cause the disc surfaces to become glazed, resulting in slippage.

2. *Drag or failure to release*—This trouble usually causes difficult shifting and gear clash especially when downshifting. The cause may be excessive clutch lever free play, warped or bent plates, stretched clutch cable, or broken or loose disc linings.

3. *Chatter or grabbing*—Check for worn or misaligned steel plate and clutch friction plates.

TRANSMISSION

Transmission problems are usually indicated by one or more of the following symptoms:

a. Difficulty shifting gears

b. Gear clash when downshifting

c. Slipping out of gear

d. Excessive noise in neutral

e. Excessive noise in gear

Transmission symptoms are sometimes hard to distinguish from clutch symptoms. Be sure the clutch is not causing the trouble before working on the transmission.

POOR HANDLING

Poor handling may be caused by improper tire pressures, a damaged frame or swinging arm, worn shocks or front forks, weak fork springs, a bent or broken steering stem, misaligned wheels, loose or missing spokes, worn tires, bent handlebar, worn wheel bearing, or dragging brakes.

BRAKE PROBLEMS

Sticking brakes may be caused by broken or weak return springs, improper cable or rod adjustment, or dry pivot and cam bushings. Grabbing brakes may be caused by greasy linings which must be replaced. Brake grab may also be due to out-of-round drums or linings which have broken loose from the brake shoes. Glazed linings will cause loss of stopping power.

ELECTRICAL PROBLEMS

Bulbs which continuously burn out may be caused by excessive vibration, loose connections that permit sudden current surges, poor battery connections, installation of the wrong type bulb, or a faulty voltage regulator.

A dead battery or one which discharges quickly may be caused by a faulty alternator or rectifier. Check for loose or corroded terminals. Shorted battery cells or broken terminals will keep a battery from charging. Low water level will decrease a battery's capacity. A battery left uncharged after installation will sulphate, rendering it useless.

A majority of light and horn or other electrical accessory problems are caused by loose or corroded ground connections. Check those first, and then substitute known good units for easier troubleshooting.

TROUBLESHOOTING GUIDE

The following summarizes the troubleshooting process. Use it to outline possible problem areas, then refer to the specific chapter or section involved.

Loss of Power

1. *Poor compression*—Check piston rings and cylinder, cylinder head gasket, and valve leaks.

2. *Overheated engine*—Check lubricating oil supply, air leaks, ignition timing, clogged cooling fins, slipping clutch, and carbon in the combustion chamber.

3. *Improper mixture*—Check for dirty air cleaner, restricted fuel flow—jets, clogged gas cap vent hole.

Gearshifting Difficulties

1. *Clutch*—Check clutch adjustment, clutch springs, friction plates, steel plates, and oil quantity and type.

2. *Transmission*—Check oil quantity and type, oil grade, gearshift mechanism adjustment, return spring, and gear change forks.

Brake Troubles

1. *Poor brakes*—Check brake adjustment, brake drum out-of-round, oil or water on brake linings, and loose brake linkage or cables.

2. *Noisy brakes*—Check for worn or scratched linings, scratched drums, and dirt in brakes.

3. *Unadjustable brakes*—Check for worn linings, drums, and brake cams.

4. *Miscellaneous*—Check for dragging brakes, tight wheel bearings, and clogged exhaust system.

Steering Problems

1. *Hard steering*—Check steering head bearings, steering stem head, and correct tire pressures.

2. *Pulls to one side*—Check for worn swinging arm bushings, bent swinging arm, bent steering head, bent frame, and front and rear wheel alignment.

3. *Shimmy*—Check for loose or missing spokes, deformed wheel rims, worn wheel bearings, and improper wheel balance.

CHAPTER THREE

PERIODIC MAINTENANCE
AND TUNE-UP

Regular maintenance is the best guarantee of a trouble-free, long-lasting motorcycle. An afternoon spent now, cleaning and adjusting, can prevent costly mechanical problems in the future, and unexpected breakdowns on the road.

The tune-up procedures presented in this chapter should hold no terror for an owner with average mechanical skills. The operations are outlined step-by-step and easy to follow.

Instruments and measuring devices calibrated to the metric system, rather than the inch-foot system, will be easier to work with when measuring parts and comparing them to the specifications, and when tightening critical-torque nuts and bolts. The text gives specifications in both systems, but inch-foot equivalents of standard metric values are occasionally awkward.

MAINTENANCE INTERVALS

The factory recommends a tune-up every 4,000 miles. The oil should be changed and minor lubrication service performed every 2,000 miles.

TOOLS AND PARTS

In addition to the basic tools suggested in Chapter One, a tune-up requires a strobe timing light—or a buzz box—and a set of flat feeler gauges, preferably calibrated in millimeters.

Parts required for a tune-up are two spark plugs, a set of points and a condenser, and 4.2 pints of oil.

SERVICING

The following pages cover servicing or replacement of oil, spark plugs, ignition breaker points and condenser, static and advanced timing, valve clearances, air cleaner, fuel valve, carburetors, clutch, and battery. The tune-up should be performed in the order that the operations are listed.

Other routine service procedures, such as adjusting the brakes, the headlight, and adjusting and lubricating the swing arm bearings and controls, are covered in other chapters.

OIL

Frequency

The engine oil should be changed every 2,000 miles, or 60 days, whichever occurs first. These recommendations assume operation in moderate climates. In extremely cold climates, change oil every 30 days regardless of the mileage. The time interval is more important than the use interval because acids formed by gasoline and water vapor from condensation will contaminate the oil even if the motorcycle is not run for several months. Also, if the motorcycle is operated under dusty conditions the oil will get dirty more quickly, so change it more frequently.

Use only a detergent oil with an API rating of SE, SD (formerly MS), or SC (formerly MM). These quality ratings are stamped on the top of the can. Always try to use the same brand of oil. The use of oil additives is not recommended.

SAE 30 oil is recommended for normal operation in moderate climates. The factory recommends the following alternate weights (see **Table 1**) according to prevailing temperatures.

Table 1   RECOMMENDED OIL

Temperature	Oil Grade
75°F and above	SAE 40
32°F to 75°F	SAE 30
32°F and below	SAE 10 W 30

Draining Oil

1. Run the engine for a few minutes. Warm oil drains faster and carries more sludge with it than cold oil.

2. Place a drip pan of at least 3 quart capacity beneath the drain plug located at the bottom rear of the oil pan. Remove the dipstick from the engine.

3. Remove the 19mm magnetic oil drain plug from the oil pan (**Figure 1**), allow the oil to drain, and clean the plug of metal particles that have been captured by the magnet.

4. Crank the engine several times with the kickstarter to force out any oil trapped in the engine's internal recesses.

NOTE: *Pour the used oil into plastic bottles, such as those used for laundry bleach. Cap tightly and discard them in the trash.*

NOTE: *US models are not equipped with a disposable oil filter cartridge. The factory recommends that at 16,000-mile intervals (every eighth oil change) the following be done:*

5. After draining the oil, remove the oil pan bolts, the oil pan, and gasket (**Figure 2**).

6. Thoroughly clean the pan with solvent.

7. Bend back the locking tabs on the 10mm nuts that hold the oil strainer in place (**Figure 3**), and remove the nuts, strainer, and gasket.

8. Wash the strainer thoroughly in solvent and reinstall it, mesh-side down. Bend the locking tabs down to secure the nuts after they have been tightened.

9. Check the gasket surface of the oil pan for flatness. If the pan is bowed or has swoops and dips around the bolt holes, carefully hammer it flat again. Replace the gasket *every* time you remove the oil pan. Use a non-hardening gasket cement on both sides of the gasket. Start *all* the pan bolts before tightening any of them. Tighten them ¼ turn past snug and *no more*. Further tightening will bend the oil pan and it will leak.

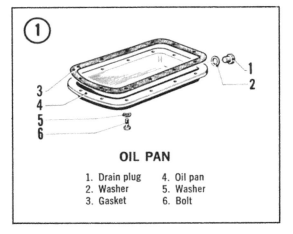

OIL PAN

1. Drain plug   4. Oil pan
2. Washer   5. Washer
3. Gasket   6. Bolt

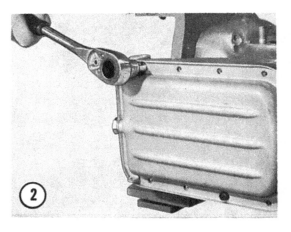

Filling With Oil

1. Install the drain plug in the oil pan.
2. Fill the engine with 4.2 pints (2 quarts, 4 ounces) of recommended oil, and check the level with the dipstick.

> NOTE: *Insert the dipstick all the way into the hole but do not screw it in when checking the level.*

3. Run the engine at about 1,000 rpm for a couple of minutes, shut it off, and check for seepage from the drain plug and around the pan gasket. Recheck the oil level with the dipstick, and top up if necessary.

TUNE-UP

A complete tune-up should be performed every 4,000 miles of normal riding (combination of highway and city). More frequent tune-ups may be required if the motorcycle is used primarily in stop-and-go city traffic.

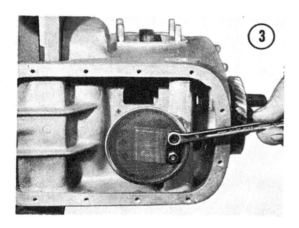

For maximum performance and fuel economy, the expendable ignition parts (spark plugs, points, and condenser) should be replaced during the tune-up and you should have them on hand before beginning. If replacement is impractical, the old parts can be reused once if their condition is satisfactory as described later.

Because different systems in an engine interact, the procedures should be done in the following order:

1. Tighten cylinder head bolts.
2. Adjust valve clearances.
3. Work on ignition system.
4. Adjust carburetors.

HEAD BOLT TORQUE AND VALVE ADJUSTMENT

Incorrect clearances between the tappets and valve stems can damage the valves and mar performance. To forestall premature wear and a costly regrind, adjust the clearances regularly.

> NOTE: *This procedure is performed with the engine cold. The factory recommends that the valves be adjusted every 4,000 miles.*

1. Unscrew the cap nuts in the center of the rocker covers, and the 2 nuts inboard of the large fins on the heads. Remove the covers, the cover gaskets, and the washers (**Figure 4**).
2. Check the torque of the cylinder head bolts (**Table 2** and **Figure 5**).

Table 2   HEAD BOLT TORQUE

Model	Tightening Torque
All	3.3-3.7 mkg (24-27 ft.-lb.)

3. Remove the spark plugs from the cylinders and rotate the crankshaft with the kickstarter until the cylinder to be adjusted is at TDC on compression. This will close both valves. The OT mark on the flywheel should line up with the reference mark in the inspection hole.
4. Check the clearances with a flat feeler gauge. The intake (rear) valve should be 0.15mm (0.006 in.) for all models, and exhaust valve

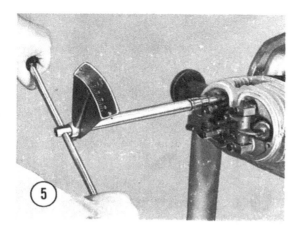

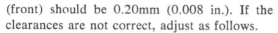

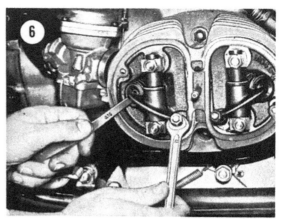

(front) should be 0.20mm (0.008 in.). If the clearances are not correct, adjust as follows.

5. Loosen the 12mm locknut (**Figure 6**). To decrease the clearance, turn the adjusting screw clockwise; to increase it, turn it counterclockwise. The gap is correct when there is a slight drag on the feeler blade.

6. When the clearance is correct, tighten the locknut and then recheck the clearance to make sure the tightening did not upset the setting.

7. The adjustment steps must be performed on both valves on each cylinder with engine at TDC.

8. Rotate the crankshaft to bring the other cylinder to TDC on compression, and check and adjust the clearances in the same manner.

9. Before reinstalling the rocker covers, fill the rocker shafts with oil (**Figure 7**), check the gaskets for damage, and replace them if necessary. Clean the sealing surfaces carefully and reinstall the covers.

SPARK PLUGS
Removal

1. Blow out any debris from the recesses around the spark plugs.

2. Carefully remove the spark plug leads. Do not jerk them; the wires could be pulled out of the insulator caps.

3. Unscrew the spark plugs with a socket that has a rubber insert to grip the insulator.

Inspection

The normal color of the spark plug insulator tip ranges from light tan to chocolate brown,

depending on the concentration of lead in the gas being used.

Figure 8 shows some abnormal tip conditions, along with probable causes.

Plug Types

Two reach-length plugs are used on all 3 US models. Short-reach plugs have a T1 suffix (e.g., W 240 T1), and long-reach plugs have a T2 suffix. See **Tables 3 and 4**.

Table 3   SPARK PLUG TYPES

Model	Plug Type
R50, R60	Bosch W 240 T1, T2*
R69	Bosch W 240 T1, T2*, during break-in
	Bosch W 260 T1, T2* after break-in
*See discussion on plug types.	

SPARK PLUG CONDITION (8)

NORMAL
• Identified by light tan or gray deposits on the firing tip.
• Can be cleaned.

GAP BRIDGED
• Identified by deposit buildup closing gap between electrodes.
• Caused by oil or carbon fouling. If deposits are not excessive, the plug can be cleaned.

OIL FOULED
• Identified by wet black deposits on the insulator shell bore electrodes.
• Caused by excessive oil entering combustion chamber through worn rings and pistons, excessive clearance between valve guides and stems, or worn or loose bearings. Can be cleaned. If engine is not repaired, use a hotter plug.

CARBON FOULED
• Identified by black, dry fluffy carbon deposits on insulator tips, exposed shell surfaces and electrodes.
• Caused by too cold a plug, weak ignition, dirty air cleaner, too rich a fuel mixture, or excessive idling. Can be cleaned.

LEAD FOULED
• Identified by dark gray, black, yellow, or tan deposits or a fused glazed coating on the insulator tip.
• Caused by highly leaded gasoline. Can be cleaned.

WORN
• Identified by severely eroded or worn electrodes.
• Caused by normal wear. Should be replaced.

FUSED SPOT DEPOSIT
• Identified by melted or spotty deposits resembling bubbles or blisters.
• Caused by sudden acceleration. Can be cleaned.

OVERHEATING
• Identified by a white or light gray insulator with small black or gray brown spots and with bluish-burnt appearance of electrodes.
• Caused by engine overheating, wrong type of fuel, loose spark plugs, too hot a plug, or incorrect ignition timing. Replace the plug.

PREIGNITION
• Identified by melted electrodes and possibly blistered insulator. Metallic deposits on insulator indicate engine damage.
• Caused by wrong type of fuel, incorrect ignition timing or advance, too hot a plug, burned valves, or engine overheating. Replace the plug.

Table 4   PLUG LENGTH

R 50 models up to (approximately) frame
   No. 647 000 - T1

R 60 models up to (approximately) frame
   No. 1 817 300 - T1

R 69 models up to (approximately) frame
   No. 664 950 - T1

All subsequent models use long-reach (T2) plugs.

NOTE: *To accurately determine the reach-length, look at the plug bores in the cylinder heads. For short-reach plugs, the plug bore is unmarked, and for long-reach plugs, the letters* LK *are embossed above the plug bores.*

Old Plugs

If the old plugs are to be used, inspect them for cracked insulators, damaged threads, or eroded electrodes. Discard both plugs if any of these conditions are present.

Cleaning

Clean the tips of the plugs with a sandblasting machine—some gas stations have them—or with a wire brush and solvent, followed by compressed air.

CAUTION
When blowing solvent and debris out of the plug with compressed air, hold the plug so the electrode end is pointed away from you.

Gapping and Installation

1. Referring to **Figure 9**, adjust the spark plug gap to 0.6mm (0.024 in.), using a wire feeler gauge. If the engine is hard to start when it is cold, close plug gap to 0.5mm (0.020 in.).

NOTE: *Vary the gap by bending only the outside electrode. The gap is correct when the gauge slips through with a slight amount of drag.*

2. Use new gaskets and screw the plugs back into the cylinder heads, turning the socket by hand until the plugs are seated. Then tighten ½ to ¾ of a turn more.

CAUTION
Overtightening can change the gap, damage the threads, prevent the gasket from sealing, and make the plug hard to remove the next time.

BREAKER POINTS

Inspection

1. Disconnect the battery ground cable to protect the ignition from a dead short during cover removal and inspection.

2. Remove the front engine cover. Two hex nuts hold the cover in place.

3. Pry open the points gently with a finger and inspect the contacts for alignment and wear. **Figure 10** shows what to look for. Replace the points if they are severely pitted or worn.

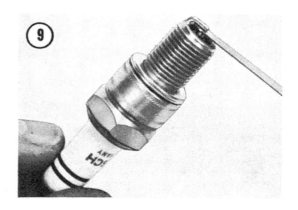

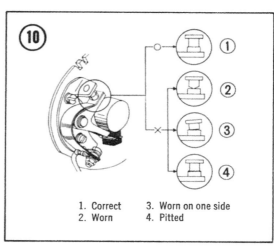

1. Correct   3. Worn on one side
2. Worn   4. Pitted

Cleaning

1. Gray discoloration is normal. Dress the contact surfaces with a point file or Flex-stone. Never use sandpaper or emery cloth; they tend to round the edges of the contacts, creating a condition that is much like extreme wear.

2. Blow away the residue, and then clean the contacts with a chemical contact cleaner, or a piece of unwaxed, stiff paper, such as a clean business card. Make certain the contact surfaces are absolutely clean. Even oil from a fingerprint can affect performance.

3. If the condition of the points is good enough for them to be reused, skip the next section outlining replacement.

Replacement

NOTE: *It is recommended that the condenser be routinely replaced along with the points. Parts are usually sold in sets.*

1. Remove the Allen bolt from the centrifugal advance mechanism and remove the mechanism from the shaft (**Figure 11**).

2. Remove points and condenser (**Figure 12**). When installing new parts be sure to install the insulating washers in their original positions.

NOTE: *The latest points being supplied have the insulating washers molded onto the fixed half of the point set. If your points have the 3-piece removable insulating washers, save these washers when you replace the points; the next set of points you buy may not have the molded-on insulator. There is no part number for the washers and they are very difficult to obtain.*

3. Unplug the wire from the point block.

4. Knead the breaker cam felt with a small quantity of distributor cam grease, and install the points and condenser. Reconnect the leads.

NOTE: *VW dealers stock a condenser that is the same Bosch number as the BMW except for the last 3 digits which are 041. This unit has the wire already soldered to it; it is the correct length, has a terminal, and is the same price as the wire-less 037 condenser. The big advantage of using the 041 is that you will not overheat and ruin a condenser trying to solder to it since the wire is already there.*

5. Lubricate the bore of the advance mechanism and the shaft with a small quantity of grease and reinstall the advance mechanism.

Adjusting the Gap

1. Rotate the crankshaft to bring the highest point of the breaker cam into contact with the breaker to open the points.

2. Loosen the lockscrew on the stationary point plate (**Figure 13**).

3. Turn the eccentric screw until the gap is between 0.35-0.40mm (0.014-0.016 in.). Refer to **Figure 14**.

4. Retighten the lockscrew and recheck the gap. If it changed when the lockscrew was tightened, reset the gap as outlined above.

NOTE: *If the engine is to be timed, do not replace the front engine cover.*

IGNITION TIMING

There are two ways to time the engine—static and the more precise method using a stroboscopic light.

The static method requires something that can signal when an electric circuit is opened and closed. This can be a buzz box, an ohmmeter, or a continuity light. The latter, more commonly called a timing light, is the easiest to use.

Such lights are available for under $2 at parts stores. A homemade light can be made from a bulb, a socket to hold it, and two wires attached to the socket with alligator clips at the ends.

Static Timing

1. Disconnect the ignition coil lead to protect the magneto from external current, and connect one lead from the timing light or buzz box to the terminal. Connect the other lead to ground (**Figure 15**).

2. With the spark plugs removed from the cylinders, rotate the engine until the "S" mark on the flywheel lines up with the reference mark on the inspection hole on the left side of the engine (**Figure 16**). This is basic timing of 9° BTC.

3. If the basic timing is correct, the timing light will light, or the buzz box will sound. Rotate the crankshaft very slightly, in both directions, past the mark. Each time the "S" passes the mark, the lamp should light or the buzzer sound.

4. If it does not, loosen the 10mm retaining nuts on either side of the magneto (**Figure 17**) and then rotate the magneto body, clockwise for advance (when viewing the magneto from the front), and counterclockwise for retard. Then retighten the 2 securing nuts on the magneto.

5. Recheck point gap and reset if necessary.

Stroboscopic Timing

Strobe timing lights are also commonly available. Beware of inexpensive ones because they usually are not very bright or durable.

1. Connect the timing light according to the instructions that are included with it. Connect cables (d) and (e) between the spark plug (a) and the high-tension lead (b). See **Figure 18**.

2. Start the engine and let it idle between 500 and 750 rpm.

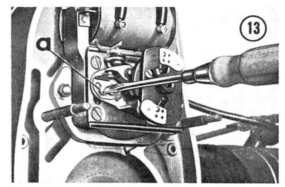

A. Lock screw

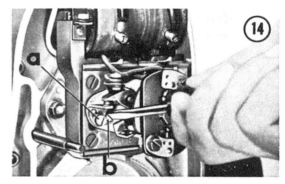

A. Lock screw
B. Eccentric screw

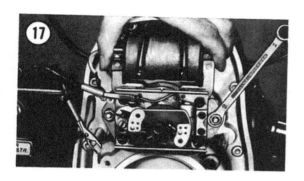

3. Hold the timing light in front of the inspection hole (**Figure 18**) perpendicular to the rotational axis of the engine. At idle, the "S" mark should appear in line with the reference mark in the inspection hole (**Figure 19**). If the "S" appears below the reference mark, the timing is too retarded (**Figure 20**).

4. Increase engine speed to about 1,200 rpm. The "S" mark should disappear upward.

5. Increase engine speed to about 5,800 rpm. The "F" mark on the flywheel should appear in the inspection hole and line up with the reference mark. When this occurs, it indicates that the ignition is in the fully advanced position.

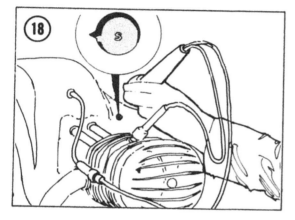

NOTE: *When the ignition timing is correct, the "S" will move up and down as engine speed is increased and decreased. If this doesn't happen, the automatic advance unit may not be working. Check the advance mechanism for free movement of the governor weights and for excessive side play of the mechanism on the shaft. If the side play is excessive, if the governor weights do not move freely, or if the advance springs do not easily return the governor weights from the outer position, the advance mechanism should be replaced. The longitudinal play of the breaker cam should be between 0.2 and 0.6mm (0.008 and 0.024 in.), and it should rotate easily.*

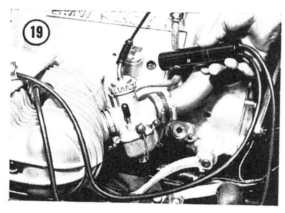

The timing difference between the two cylinders must be within ±2°. If it is not, check the cone seat of the advance mechanism for roughness. If roughness exists, it can be removed with pumice grinding paste. The maximum allowable out-of-round cone is 0.02mm (0.0007 in.) as determined with an inside micrometer. If the tolerance is excessive, replace the advance mechanism.

Check the safety spark gap between the high-tension terminals on the ignition coil and the ground tips. The gap must be between 10-11mm (0.39-0.43 in.). If it is not, carefully bend the tips with a spark plug gapper until the setting is correct (g, **Figure 21**).

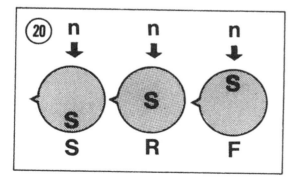

AIR CLEANER

A properly functioning air cleaner filter is essential to engine efficiency, long life, and good gas mileage. The filter should be cleaned every 4,000 miles under normal conditions and more frequently if the motorcycle is operated under dusty conditions. The filter should be changed every 8,000 miles—more frequently under dusty conditions.

1. Referring to **Figure 22**, unscrew the hand screw from the top of the filter canister and remove the canister and filter.

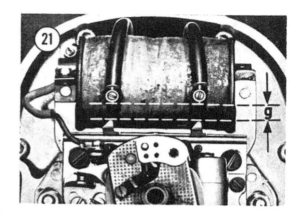

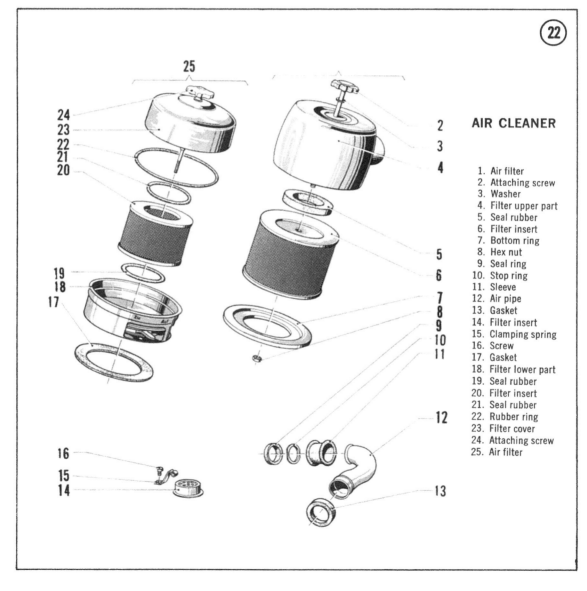

AIR CLEANER

1. Air filter
2. Attaching screw
3. Washer
4. Filter upper part
5. Seal rubber
6. Filter insert
7. Bottom ring
8. Hex nut
9. Seal ring
10. Stop ring
11. Sleeve
12. Air pipe
13. Gasket
14. Filter insert
15. Clamping spring
16. Screw
17. Gasket
18. Filter lower part
19. Seal rubber
20. Filter insert
21. Seal rubber
22. Rubber ring
23. Filter cover
24. Attaching screw
25. Air filter

2. Remove filter from canister (**Figure 23**).

3. Tap the filter lightly and blow through it to dislodge dust.

CAUTION
Do not use high-pressure compressed air to blow dust from the filter.

4. Reinstall the filter on the engine.

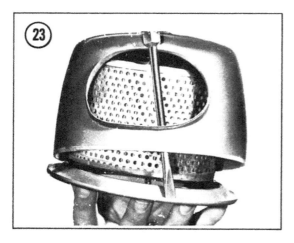

NOTE: *Make sure the bottom seal ring rests flat on the transmission housing so that the seal will be airtight when the canister is tightened completely down.*

FUEL DELIVERY

Figure 24 is an exploded view of the fuel tap that controls the flow of fuel to the carburetors. It is important that the filter screen be periodically cleaned. The float bowl should also be inspected during this procedure.

1. Make sure there is gas in the tank, and then turn off the fuel valve.

2. Disconnect the fuel lines at the carburetors and put the ends of the lines in a can to catch the fuel.

3. Turn the fuel tap on. Fuel should flow into the can.

4. Turn the tap to the RESERVE position. Fuel should flow.

5. Turn the tap to the OFF position. Fuel should cease to flow.

NOTE: *If fuel does not flow at ON or RESERVE positions, check the lines for kinks. If fuel flows with the tap in the OFF position, the valve packing is defective.*

6. Reattach the hoses to the carburetors. Make sure the fuel tap is OFF.

7. Hold the 24mm nut at the top of the valve with a wrench and unscrew the 24mm nut beneath the valve.

CAUTION
The fuel tap threads into the top nut with a left-hand thread. Should you have need to remove the fuel tap from the tank, first make sure the tank is empty and then unscrew the tap clockwise.

8. Remove the filter and clean it thoroughly in gasoline. Also clean and inspect the gasket. If it is damaged or excessively compressed, replace it.

9. Reinstall the strainer, gasket, and lower T-fitting, and carefully tighten.

10. Reinstall the lower unit in the fuel tap and tighten carefully.

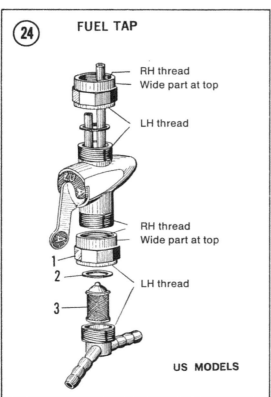

FUEL TAP

RH thread
Wide part at top

LH thread

RH thread
Wide part at top

1

2

LH thread

3

US MODELS

11. Reattach the carburetor hoses to the ends of the T-fittings.

FLOAT LEVEL

The float valve maintains a constant fuel level in the float bowl on the side of the carburetor to supply the demands of the engine at all engine speeds. As the chamber fills with fuel, the float rises, thereby pushing the valve needle into the valve to shut off the incoming fuel. As the fuel level drops, so does the needle, permitting fuel to flow into the bowl and replenish the supply.

> NOTE: *On most models, the float level is not adjustable. They can be identified by the location of the fuel line; if the fuel line enters the center of the float chamber, the carburetor has the old type, non-adjustable float. If the fuel line entry is offset, the carburetor is the newer type, and can be adjusted if necessary.*

1. Remove the screws (arrows, **Figure 25**) from the cover on top of the float bowl and take off the cover. Remove the float by lifting it out.

2. Check the float bowls for sediment and flush them with solvent.

3. Correct float height is measured between the bottom of the float lever and the cover flange where it mates with the float bowl. The distance should be 22mm (0.87 in.).

4. Adjust the setting, if necessary, by carefully bending the float lever.

5. Reinstall the floats and the float bowl covers. Make sure the float rod is centered in the recess of each cover before putting in the screws and tightening them.

CARBURETOR

To properly clean and service the carburetors they must be removed from the engine and disassembled. Before beginning, turn the fuel tap off.

1. Unscrew the screws of each of the hose clamps which secure the coupling hose between the carburetors and the air inlet tubes. Slide the rubber couplings up onto the inlet tubes, clear of the carburetor intake.

2. Unscrew the knurled rings on the top of the carburetors, and pull the throttle slides up and out of the carburetors.

3. Remove the fuel lines from the carburetors.

4. Remove the carburetors from their respective cylinders.

5. Remove the float bowl cover, the float, the needle jet, the main jet, and the idling mixture screw. See **Figure 26**.

6. Blow out all the jets and passages with compressed air and thoroughly wipe all the parts clean. Reassemble with new sealing gaskets.

7. Reinstall the carburetors, reattach the fuel lines and the breather pipes.

Adjustment

1. Turn the idling mixture screw all the way in and then back it out 2 full turns.

2. Twist the twist grip to the idling stop position and adjust both throttle cables for end play. It

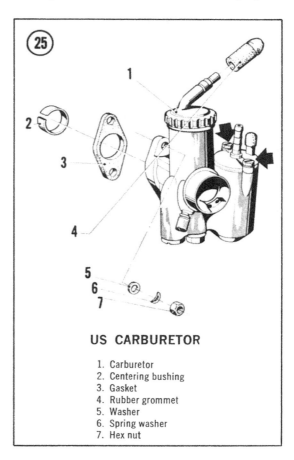

(25)

US CARBURETOR

1. Carburetor
2. Centering bushing
3. Gasket
4. Rubber grommet
5. Washer
6. Spring washer
7. Hex nut

should be approximately 1mm (0.039 in.). To make this adjustment, back off the jam nut (**Figure 27**) and turn the adjuster screw in or out until the end play is correct. Retighten the jam nut. Check the adjustment by pulling lightly on the cable sheath. It should move 1mm.

3. The idling mixture of each carburetor is set individually. To determine the engine's response to adjustment, it is necessary to remove the high-tension lead from the spark plug on the cylinder opposite the one being adjusted. Start the engine and remove the lead from the right cylinder and adjust the left carburetor as follows.

4. Slowly turn the idling mixture screw clockwise (**Figure 28**) until the engine begins to run rough. Then turn it slowly counterclockwise (it

will begin to run smoothly again) until it runs rough once again. What you are after is an optimum point which lies approximately halfway between the rich and lean rough running conditions. If the extremes occur 2 turns apart, for example, then you should turn the idling screw one turn from either extreme. This procedure requires patience and close attention to the sound of the engine.

5. When you are satisfied that you have found the correct idle mixture position, tighten the jam nut on the screw.

6. Now adjust the throttle limit screw for a smooth idle. Again, judgment is required to determine the best idling speed. Clockwise rotation of the screw will increase the idling speed and counterclockwise rotation will decrease it.

7. Replace the high-tension lead on the right-hand cylinder, remove the lead from the left-hand cylinder, and adjust the right carburetor in the same manner as the left.

CLUTCH

If the clutch slips when engaged, or if the motorcycle creeps forward when in gear, even with the clutch disengaged, the free play on the clutch control is out of adjustment.

1. To adjust, move the throw-out lever (located on the gearbox) forward by hand. See **Figure 29**. An increase in pressure should be felt when the lever has moved about 5mm (0.2 in.).

Adjuster and lock (arrows)

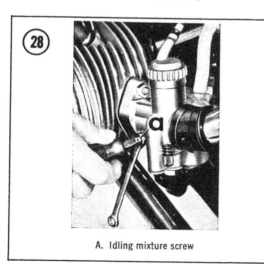

A. Idling mixture screw

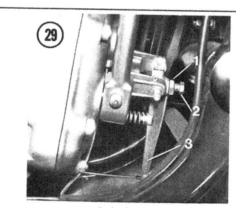

1. Locknut
2. Adjuster screw
3. Throwout lever

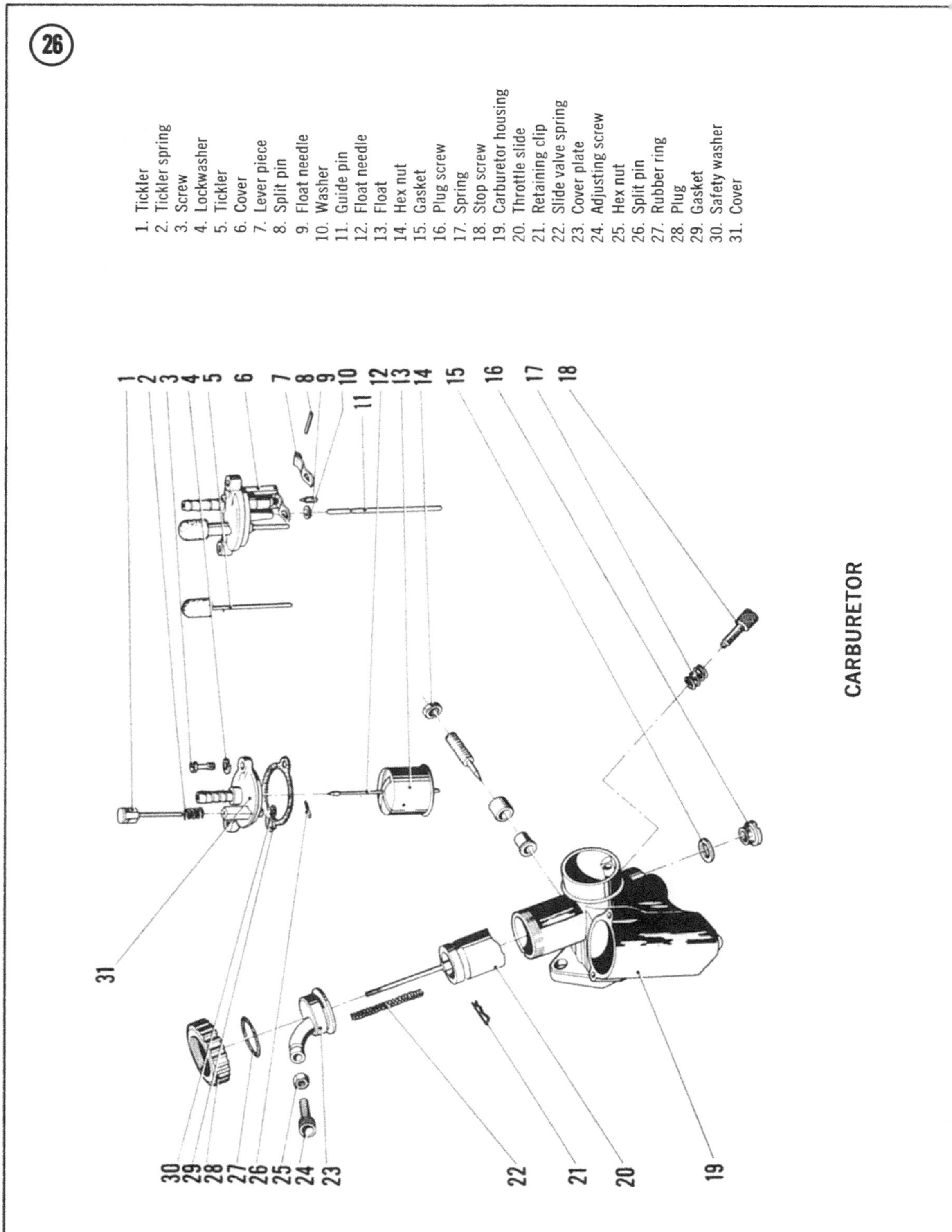

26

1. Tickler
2. Tickler spring
3. Screw
4. Lockwasher
5. Tickler
6. Cover
7. Lever piece
8. Split pin
9. Float needle
10. Washer
11. Guide pin
12. Float needle
13. Float
14. Hex nut
15. Gasket
16. Plug screw
17. Spring
18. Stop screw
19. Carburetor housing
20. Throttle slide
21. Retaining clip
22. Slide valve spring
23. Cover plate
24. Adjusting screw
25. Hex nut
26. Split pin
27. Rubber ring
28. Plug
29. Gasket
30. Safety washer
31. Cover

CARBURETOR

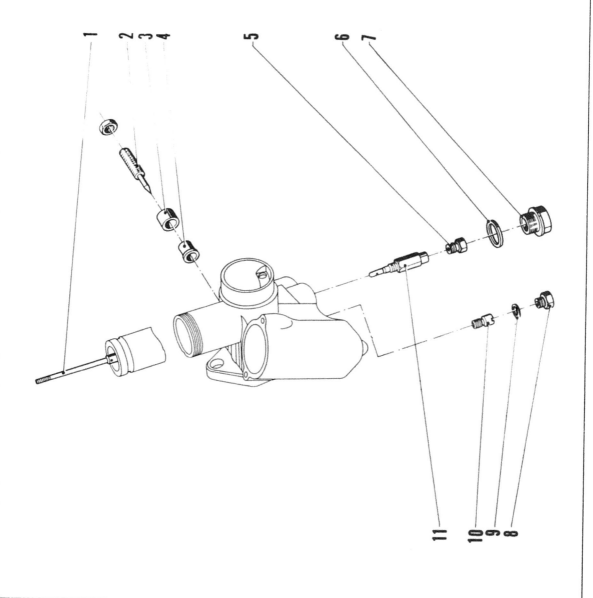

1. Jet needle
2. Air regulating screw
3. Cap
4. Sleeve
5. Main jet
6. Gasket
7. Plug
8. Plug
9. Gasket
10. Idling jet
11. Needle jet

2. If the free play is less than that specified above, loosen the knurled locknut at the hand lever end of the cable, and turn the cable adjuster in—clockwise—until the end play is correct. Retighten the knurled locknut.

3. If the free play is greater than that specified above, turn the cabe adjuster out—counterclockwise—until the end play is correct, and retighten the knurled locknut.

> NOTE: *If correct free play cannot be obtained with the above procedure, proceed as follows.*

4. Turn the hand lever adjuster all the way in.

5. Undo the locknut on the adjuster bolt in the end of the throw-out lever and screw the adjuster bolt in or out until the clearance, at the hand lever, is approximately 5mm (0.2 in.).

6. Tighten the locknut on the adjuster bolt.

7. Recheck the free play at the hand lever and turn the adjuster screw out, if necessary, until it is correct. Then retighten the knurled locknut on the hand lever.

BATTERY

The battery is the heart of the electrical system. It should be checked and serviced regularly. The majority of electrical system troubles can be attributed to the neglect of this vital component.

CAUTION
Do not spill battery electrolyte on painted or polished surfaces. The liquid is highly corrosive and will damage the finish.

1. Back off the bolts retaining the seat side brackets, unscrew the front bolt from the bottom of the seat, and lift it off.

2. Unfasten the rubber hold-down strap and remove the cover.

3. Remove the 3 inspection and fill plugs from the top of the battery and visually check the level of the electrolyte. İt should be up to the bottom of the fill pipes. If the level is not correct, add distilled water.

CAUTION
Add only distilled water; do not add electrolyte.

4. Inspect battery terminals for condition and tightness. Flush off any oxidation with a solution of baking soda and water to neutralize acid in electrolyte. Lightly coat terminals with Vaseline or silicon grease to retard corrosion.

EARLES FRONT FORKS

The front wheel bearings and swinging arm pivot bearings should be cleaned and repacked with grease every 20,000 miles. Refer to Chapter Eight, *Swinging Arm — Reassembly*, and Chapter Eleven, *Bearings*.

TELESCOPIC FRONT FORKS
Damping Oil

The damping oil in the front forks should be changed every 8,000 miles or once a year, or if excessive bouncing of the front end indicates a low oil level. Each fork leg must contain exactly 280cc (0.6 pints) of oil for front suspension to operate correctly. Use Shell 4001 shock absorber oil, Belray 5W, or BP Olex 2463.

If, after oil change, front suspension continues to bounce or "hobby-horse," major service may be required. See Chapter Eight.

> NOTE: *The filling capacity of fork legs after disassembly is 280cc. When refilling legs during oil change, pour 265cc of oil into each leg.*

1. Place the motorcycle on the centerstand to extend the fork legs. Remove the rubber cap from the bottom of each fork leg.

2. Place a drip pan beneath one of the fork legs. Hold the 4mm Allen bolt to prevent it from turning and unscrew the 13mm plug (**Figure 30**).

3. Unscrew the fill plug from the top of the fork leg with the pin wrench provided in the motorcycle tool kit (**Figure 31**). Allow several minutes for the fork leg to drain, and then drain the opposite leg in the same manner.

4. Reinstall the drain plugs and the rubber plugs in the bottom of the fork legs.

5. Fill each fork leg with 265cc of a recommended fork oil. Install fill plugs and tighten.

FINAL DRIVE

The oil level in the final drive should be

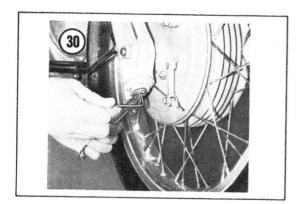

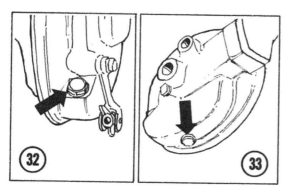

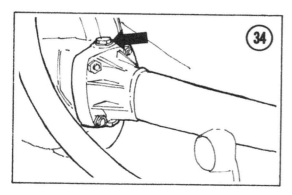

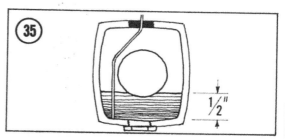

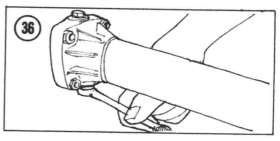

checked at each oil change. The oil level should be up to the bottom of the threads in the fill-plug opening with the motorcycle on the centerstand. See **Figure 32**.

The final drive oil should be changed every 5,000 miles. Unscrew the drain plug (**Figure 33**) and allow at least 15 minutes for the oil to drain. Then screw in and tighten the plug and fill the final drive with ¼ liter (0.44 Imp. pint or 0.53 U.S. pint) of SAE 90 hypoid gear oil.

> NOTE: *Before draining the final drive oil, ride the motorcycle for several miles to warm up the drive and oil so that it will drain freely.*

DRIVE SHAFT

The oil level in the drive shaft should be checked each time the final drive oil level is checked. Unscrew the top fill plug (**Figure 34**) and insert a drift, a file, or a piece of stiff wire. The level should be as shown in **Figure 35**. The drive shaft, like the final drive, uses SAE 90 hypoid gear oil.

The drive shaft oil should be changed every 5,000 miles. With the oil warm, unscrew the drain plug (**Figure 36**) and allow about 15 minutes for the oil to drain. Screw in the drain plug and pour 0.1 liter (0.17 Imp. pint or 0.21 U.S. pint) of oil in through the fill plug opening. Install the fill plug and tighten it securely.

CHAPTER FOUR

ENGINE

To remove the engine, it is necessary to remove the transmission (see Chapter Five) and the drive train (see Chapter Eleven). Refer to these chapters, perform the necessary steps, and continue as follows.

> **CAUTION**
> *Disconnect the battery. If you attempt to remove the front cover without disconnecting the battery, it is likely that the cover will short against electrical connections.*

Removal

1. Turn off the fuel tap and remove the hoses from the carburetors.

2. Unscrew the carburetor covers and remove them and slides from carburetors (**Figure 1**).

3. Unscrew the exhaust pipe connector rings with a pin wrench (BMW tool No. 338/ for R 50 and R 60, No. 338/2 for R 69). See **Figure 2**.

> NOTE: *When reinstalling the exhaust pipes, the threads on the exhaust flanges and connector rings must be coated with coarse, dry graphite grease.*

4. Remove the 19mm nuts from the ends of the rear engine mounting rod (**Figure 3**).

5. With a soft-face mallet, tap the rod to the right and remove the left exhaust pipe clamp and footrest. Then, tap the rod to the left and remove the right clamp and footrest.

6. Loosen the rear exhaust pipe mounts and remove the entire exhaust system.

7. Disconnect the fuel line Tee from the bottom of the fuel tap (**Figure 4**).

8. Remove the 2 hex nuts from the front engine cover and remove the cover.

9. Refer to **Figure 5** and remove the black, red, blue, and brown wires from their terminals and the black/red wire from the ignition coil.

10. Lift the springs off the generator brushes, slide the brushes halfway out of their holders, and jam them in place with the springs. See **Figure 6**.

11. Unscrew the two 5mm Allen screws which hold the generator to the engine, and remove the generator body.

> NOTE: *Some engines are fitted with a centering washer and have three 6mm holes in the front of the engine (**Figure 7**). Carefully remove the washer and save it for reinstallation. Also, the hole to the breather passage must be plugged with a M6 x 10 screw fitted with a flat aluminum washer.*

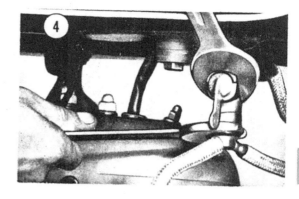

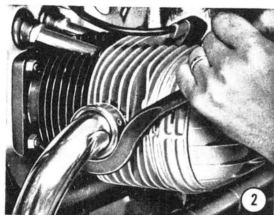

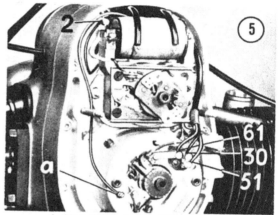

1. Black (30)   3. Blue (61)   5. Black/red (2)
2. Red (51)   4. Brown (a)

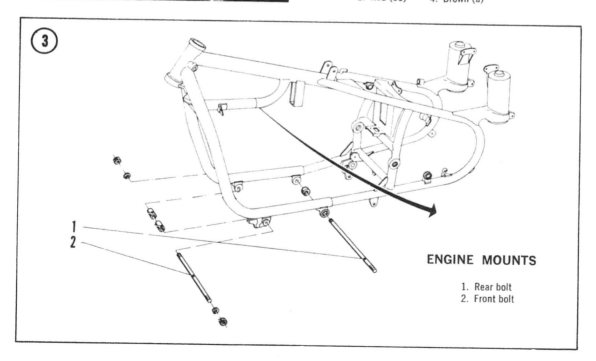

ENGINE MOUNTS

1. Rear bolt
2. Front bolt

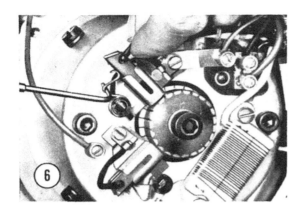

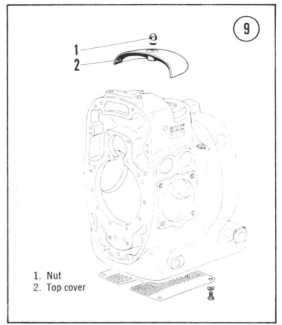

1. Nut
2. Top cover

Breather plug (arrow)

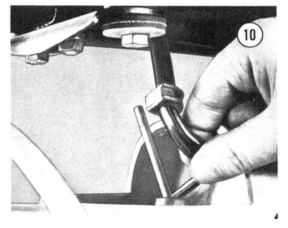

12. Remove the 6mm Allen screw from the end of the armature (**Figure 8**).

13. Place the armature back into the generator body, wrap them in clean paper, and store them out of the way.

14. Remove the top cover from the engine (**Figure 9**).

15. Carefully pull the wiring harness out of the engine (**Figure 10**).

16. Remove the bolt holding the top engine mount to the frame clamp (**Figure 11**).

17. Place a box beneath the engine and remove the 19mm hex nuts from the ends of the lower front mounting bolt.

18. Tap the bottom mounting bolts all the way out—first the rear and then the front. Remove the spacers—front and rear—from the left side of the engine (**Figure 12**).

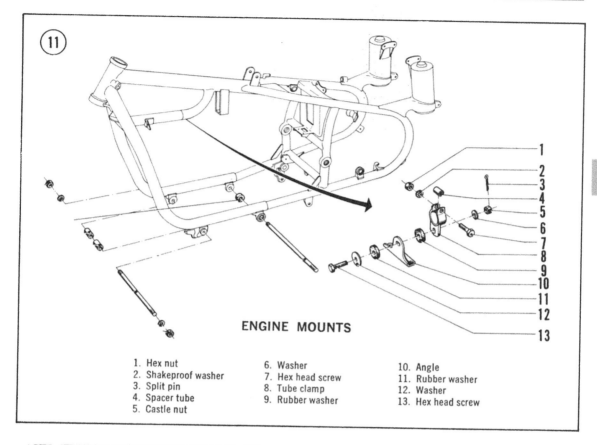

ENGINE MOUNTS

1. Hex nut
2. Shakeproof washer
3. Split pin
4. Spacer tube
5. Castle nut

6. Washer
7. Hex head screw
8. Tube clamp
9. Rubber washer

10. Angle
11. Rubber washer
12. Washer
13. Hex head screw

19. Tilt the engine carefully forward and lift it out of the frame, to the right.

CAUTION
Be careful not to let the automatic advance unit on the ignition hit the frame as the engine is removed.

ENGINE INSTALLATION

Installation of the engine should follow the respective removal procedures in reverse. Reread the steps as you go and do not try to do it from memory; even if just a couple of days have passed since you removed the engine, there is still a good chance that a vital step will be overlooked.

CAMSHAFT AND TIMING GEARS

Disassembly

The camshaft is gear driven and mounted above the crankshaft. **Figures 13 and 14** are exploded views of the camshaft and valve operating mechanism.

1. Remove the oil drain plug from the engine and allow the oil to drain.

2. Remove the distributor rotor and the magneto from the engine (**Figure 15**).

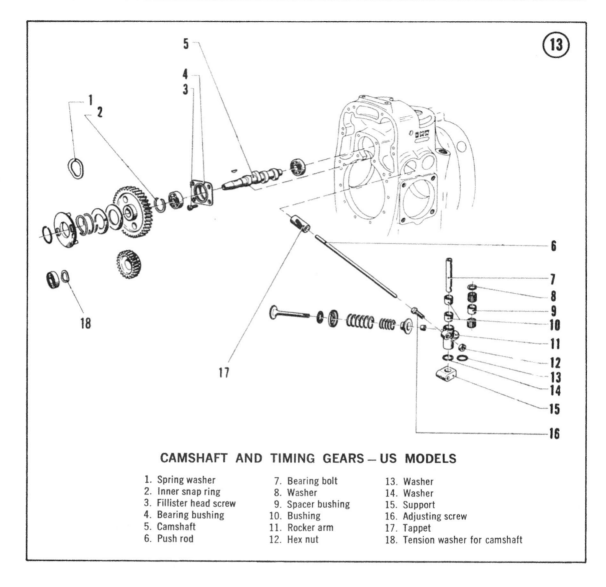

CAMSHAFT AND TIMING GEARS – US MODELS

1. Spring washer
2. Inner snap ring
3. Fillister head screw
4. Bearing bushing
5. Camshaft
6. Push rod
7. Bearing bolt
8. Washer
9. Spacer bushing
10. Bushing
11. Rocker arm
12. Hex nut
13. Washer
14. Washer
15. Support
16. Adjusting screw
17. Tappet
18. Tension washer for camshaft

3. Insert a hard steel rod, ⅛ in. diameter, 2⅛ in. long, in the hole. Screw in the rotor bolt, hold the rotor, and tighten the bolt to remove the rotor (**Figure 16**). Place the rotor in the magneto, wrap them in clean paper, and store them in a safe place.

4. Remove the 12 Allen screws, located inside the mating flange around the circumference of the timing cover. Use a rubber or plastic mallet and tap the timing cover off gently.

5. Remove the breather valve, the spring ring, and the shim from the front of the crankshaft (**Figure 17**).

NOTE: *On early models, it is necessary first to remove the snap ring from the camshaft gear before removing the breather plate and the pressure spring.*

CAUTION
When reinstalling the breather plate, make sure its face is flat and smooth. Oil it liberally before reinstalling the cover.

6. Rotate the camshaft timing gear to line up the holes with 2 of the screws which hold the camshaft bearing block in place (**Figure 18**).

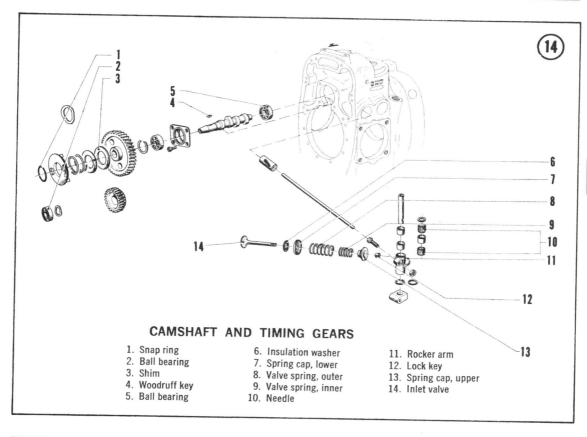

CAMSHAFT AND TIMING GEARS

1. Snap ring
2. Ball bearing
3. Shim
4. Woodruff key
5. Ball bearing
6. Insulation washer
7. Spring cap, lower
8. Valve spring, outer
9. Valve spring, inner
10. Needle
11. Rocker arm
12. Lock key
13. Spring cap, upper
14. Inlet valve

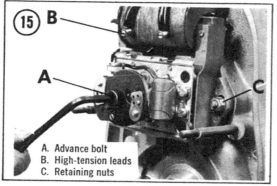

A. Advance bolt
B. High-tension leads
C. Retaining nuts

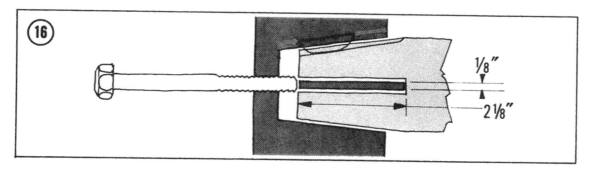

With an impact driver, remove the screws and rotate the gear to line up the holes with the other 2 screws and remove these.

7. Install the puller (BMW tool No. 355a) by first slacking off the 22mm nut, and then screwing the threaded end of the puller into the front of the camshaft. Hold the end of the puller bolt with a wrench and turn the nut clockwise to remove the camshaft, gear, and bearing block (**Figure 19**). If the tool is not available, heat the case to about 180°F and *carefully* pry the camshaft assembly out with rounded pry bars or tire irons.

> NOTE: *If the gear and bearing are in good condition, it is a good idea to leave the camshaft, bearing, and gear assembled.*

8. If the camshaft gear or front bearing needs replacing, heat the gear and support the rear face of it on 2 horizontal wooden blocks. Carefully tap out the camshaft with a soft-face mallet.

9. Remove the snap ring which holds the bearing in the bearing block, support the bearing block on 2 wooden blocks, and carefully tap the camshaft out of the bearing and block. See **Figure 20**.

> CAUTION
> *When reinstalling the camshaft assembly, first heat the engine block to about 200°F. Also, be sure the timing marks on the camshaft gear and the crankshaft drive gear are lined up before the camshaft assembly is tapped into place.*

CYLINDER HEAD

Disassembly

The cylinder heads can be removed from the engine with the engine installed in the chassis. **Figures 21 and 22** are exploded views of the cylinder head assemblies and the cylinders.

1. Refer to the discussion on removing the engine in this chapter and remove the carburetors and exhaust system.

2. Place a drip pan beneath the head being removed.

3. Unscrew the cap nuts in the center of the rocker cover (**Figure 23**), remove the two 10mm nuts located inboard of the larger fins on the heads (**Figure 24**) and remove the rocker covers.

> CAUTION
> *On R 69 models, remove the 2 bolts and washers (**Figure 25**).*

4. Pull off the high-tension lead from the spark plug and remove the plug.

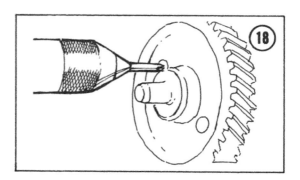

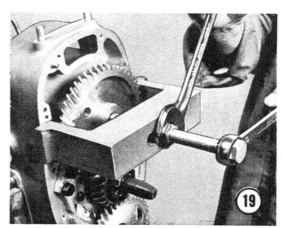

5. Unscrew the hex head bolts from the rocker shaft supports (**Figure 26**), and remove the supports, the rockers, and the pushrods.

6. Install the cylinder head in BMW fixture No. 5034 (this special tool has an integral valve spring compressor). Compress the springs and

remove the valve keepers with either a small magnet or a scribe (**Figure 27**). Remove the top cap, the springs, the bottom spring cap, and the insulation washer.

7. Remove the head from the fixture, turn it over, and remove the valves.

Inspection

1. Check the cylinder head for cracks, and for smoothness along the sealing surface. Clean carbon deposits from the combustion chamber with a soft wire brush.

CAUTION
Do not scrape carbon from head. Hard, sharp-edge tools will scar aluminum surface of combustion chamber and create burrs which will cause hot spots during engine operation.

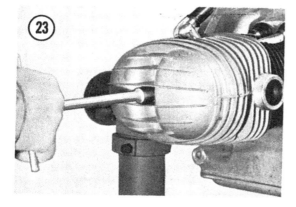

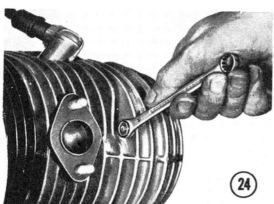

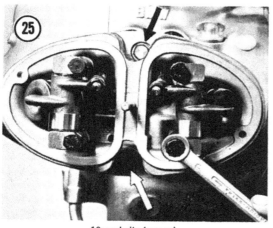
10mm bolts (arrows)

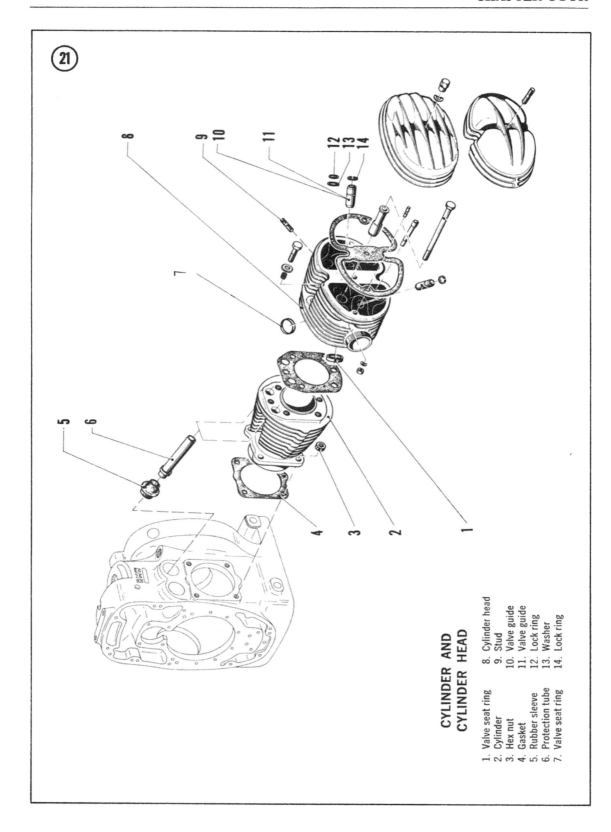

㉑

**CYLINDER AND
CYLINDER HEAD**

1. Valve seat ring
2. Cylinder
3. Hex nut
4. Gasket
5. Rubber sleeve
6. Protection tube
7. Valve seat ring
8. Cylinder head
9. Stud
10. Valve guide
11. Valve guide
12. Lock ring
13. Washer
14. Lock ring

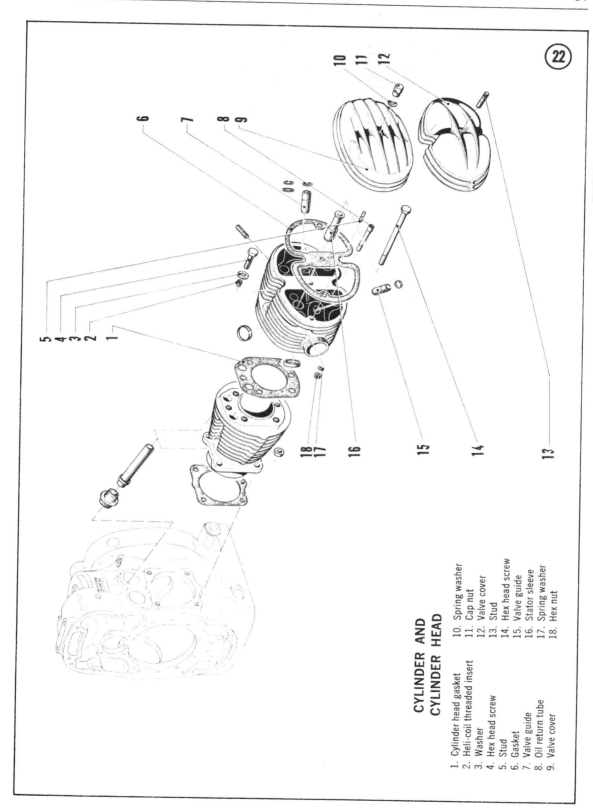

**CYLINDER AND
CYLINDER HEAD**

1. Cylinder head gasket
2. Heli-coil threaded insert
3. Washer
4. Hex head screw
5. Stud
6. Gasket
7. Valve guide
8. Oil return tube
9. Valve cover
10. Spring washer
11. Cap nut
12. Valve cover
13. Stud
14. Hex head screw
15. Valve guide
16. Stator sleeve
17. Spring washer
18. Hex nut

22

2. Refer to **Figure 28** for measurement of the clearance between the valve stem and its guide. Insert the valve into the guide and use a dial indicator to measure the clearance for both the "X" and "Y" dimensions. If the clearance is more than specified in **Table 1**, the valve and its guide should be replaced as a set.

Table 1   VALVE STEM CLEARANCE

Model	Clearance
R 50, R 60 (7mm diameter stem)	
Intake	0.10mm (0.004 in.)
Exhaust	0.15mm (0.006 in.)
R 69S (8mm stem diameter)	
Intake	0.15mm (0.006 in.)
Exhaust	0.2mm (0.008 in.)

3. Grind the old valve guide top down to the snap ring and remove the snap ring (**Figure 29**).

4. Heat the cylinder head to 360-428°F and tap the guide out of the head, into the combustion chamber, with the drift punch (BMW tool No. 5127 or 5128). See **Figure 30**.

5. Press a new valve guide, with the snap ring installed, into the head from the top, while the head is still hot.

> NOTE: *The interference fit of the guide into the head should be 0.025-0.030mm (0.0009-0.0012 in.). If the correct fit cannot be obtained, a 1mm oversize guide, machined to the correct fit, must be used.*

6. Allow the head and guide to cool and ream the valve guide with a 7K7 reamer for 7mm internal-diameter guides, or an 8H7 reamer for the 8mm internal-diameter guides (**Figure 31**). The valve guide internal-diameter is given in **Table 2**.

Table 2   VALVE GUIDE INTERNAL DIAMETER

Valve Size	Internal Diameter
7mm Intake	7.050-7.065mm (0.2776-0.2781 in.)
7mm Exhaust	7.065-7.080mm (0.2781-0.2787 in.)
8mm Intake	8.050-8.065mm (0.3169-0.3175 in.)
8mm Exhaust	8.065-8.080mm (0.3175-0.3181 in.)

7. Measure the vertical runout of the valve face with a dial indicator as shown in **Figure 32**. If runout is more than 0.03mm (0.0012 in.), replace the valve.

8. Measure the width of the contact surface on the valve head (**Figure 33** and **Table 3**). If it is more than specified, replace the valve.

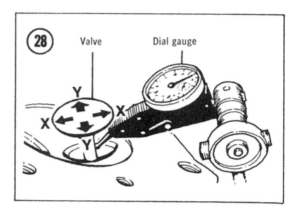

(28)   Valve   Dial gauge

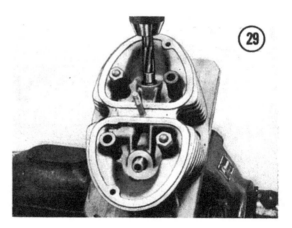

(29)

(30)

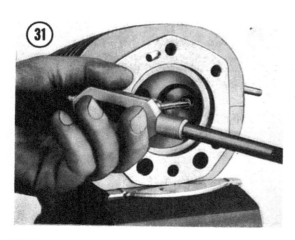

Dial indicator

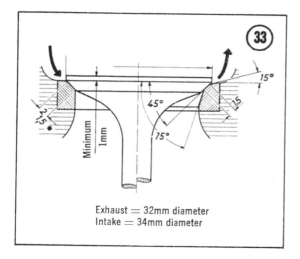

Exhaust = 32mm diameter
Intake = 34mm diameter

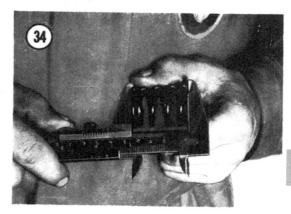

Table 3   VALVE HEAD CONTACT SURFACE

Model	Contact Surface Width
R 50. R 60	
Intake	1.5mm (0.0590 in.)
Exhaust	2.0mm (0.0787 in.)
R 69	
Both	1.5mm (0.0590 in.)

9. Check the edge of the valve for burned spots and replace it if necessary.

10. Check to see if the valve is seating in the head correctly. If it is not seating completely, the valve seats must be reground. This is a job for a machine shop.

11. Measure the free height of the valve springs with a vernier caliper (**Figure 34**) and measure the force required to compress the springs. Replace any which do not conform to the values in **Table 4**.

12. Measure the support area of the rocker arm shaft with an outside micrometer, and the diameter of the rocker arm bushing with an inside micrometer (**Figure 35**). The clearance should not be greater than 0.045mm (0.0018 in.). If it is, one or both of the parts must be replaced.

Table 4   VALVE SPRING DIMENSIONS

Valve Spring	Free Length	Installed Length	Spring Force (Installed)
Inner Spring—R 50. R 60	37.5mm (1.4763 in.)	30.5mm (1.2007 in.)	16.5 lb.
R 69S	42.0mm (1.6536 in.)	35.0mm (1.3779 in.)	24.0 lb.
Outer Spring—R 50. R 60	42.3mm (1.6654 in.)	34.0mm (1.3386 in.)	41.0 lb.
R 69S	43.25mm (1.7028 in.)	35.0mm (1.3779 in.)	42.3 lb.

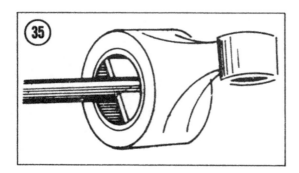

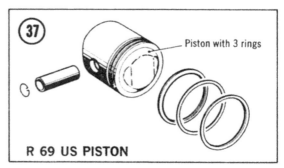

R 69 US PISTON

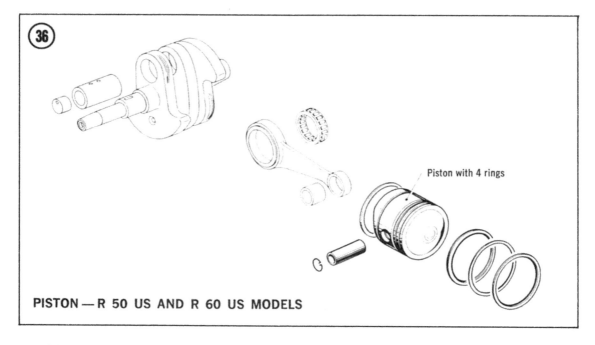

Piston with 3 rings

Piston with 4 rings

PISTON — R 50 US AND R 60 US MODELS

13. Check each rocker arm for cracks, and the running surfaces for pits and galling. If any of these conditions exist, replace the affected rocker.

Reassembly

1. Reassemble the head in reverse order, referring to the exploded views for the sequence of the parts, and install the cylinder head on the engine.

2. Set the valve tappet clearances according to the instructions in Chapter Three.

PISTON AND CYLINDER

The piston assembly for R 50 and R 60 models (shown in **Figure 36**) has a compression ring on top, a secondary compression ring immediately below, and two oil scraper rings, one above the wrist pin and one below. The piston assembly for the R 69 (shown in **Figure 37**) has a compression ring, a secondary compression ring, and one oil scraper ring above the wrist pin.

The following procedure can be performed with the engine installed in the chassis.

1. Remove the cylinder head as described in this chapter.

2. Unscrew the four 14mm nuts at the base of the cylinder (**Figure 38**), and remove the head gasket, the cylinder, and the base gasket.

3. Place wooden protection blocks between the piston and the crankcase.

4. With an awl or small screwdriver, remove

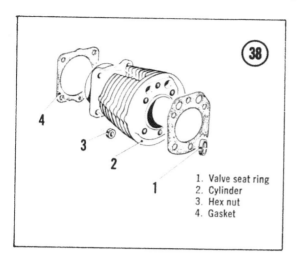

1. Valve seat ring
2. Cylinder
3. Hex nut
4. Gasket

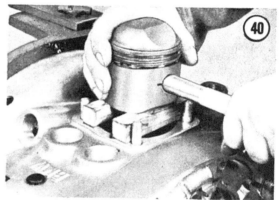

both snap rings from piston (**Figure 39**). Be very careful not to drop the clips into the crankcase.

5. Press out the wrist pin with a pin extractor, or a drift (BMW tool No. 5129). See **Figure 40**. If the pin will not move, it may be necessary to heat the piston evenly with a propane or similar small torch. Remove the piston from the connecting rod.

6. Remove the rings from the piston.

Inspection

1. Use an inside micrometer as shown in **Figure 41** to measure the bore. Measure at three points: at about 10mm (0.39 in.) from the top of the cylinder, at the middle, and near the bottom. Measure first in one axis, such as in line with the wrist pin, then measure in a second axis, 90 degrees to the first. Two things are learned from this procedure—bore taper and out-of-roundness. See **Table 5**. If taper or out-of-roundness exceed the maximum allowable dimensions, the cylinder must be bored to the next oversize and new pistons fitted.

2. Measure the piston diameter at the bottom of the skirt, 90 degrees from the wrist pin holes

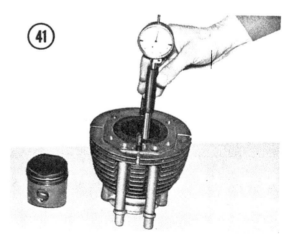

(**Figure 42**). Subtract the dimensions of the piston from the dimension of the bore, at the cylinder flange. If the difference (total wear of piston and cylinder) is greater than 0.12mm (0.0046 in.), the cylinder must be rebored to the next oversize and new pistons fitted. See **Table 6**.

Table 5   CYLINDER BORE SPECIFICATIONS

Maximum Allowable Taper (Top Diameter Smaller)	Maximum Allowable Out-of-roundness
0.03mm (0.0012 in.)	0.01mm (0.0004 in.)

Table 6   OVERSIZE PISTON SIZES

Cylinder Bore	R 50	R 60, R 69S
Standard	68.00mm (2.6772 in.)	72.00mm (2.8346 in.)
First oversize	68.50mm (2.6968 in.)	72.50mm (2.8543 in.)
Second oversize	69.00mm (2.7165 in.)	73.00mm (2.8740 in.)

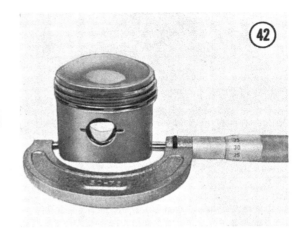

NOTE: *If a rebore is called for, the new pistons must be obtained first. It is virtually impossible to manufacture all of a given size piston to the exact same dimensions. As a result, manufacturers grade their pistons to indicate size differences from normal.*

3. Carefully scrape or wire brush the carbon from the top of the piston and the ring grooves. If the grooves are damaged or worn, the piston should be replaced.

4. Measure the end gap of the rings by placing them in the cylinder, one at a time, and check them with a feeler gauge (**Figure 43**). The ring end gap should be between 0.25 and 0.40mm (0.0098 and 0.0157 in.). Replace the rings as a set if the gap is greater than the maximum allowable.

5. Use a feeler gauge to measure the clearances between the rings and the ring lands (**Figure 44**). If the clearances are greater than the standard values (**Table 7**), replace the rings.

Table 7   PISTON RING SIDE CLEARANCES

Model	Ring
All	0.07-0.10mm (0.0028-0.0040 in.)

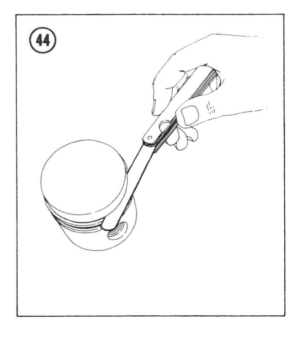

6. Measure the diameter of the piston pin, at the ends, with a micrometer. Then measure the pin bore in the piston with an inside micrometer. The difference should be between 0.0 and 0.006mm (0.0 and 0.0002 in.). If it is not, the piston and pin should be replaced.

NOTE: *Piston and pin sets are matched, and marked with either white or black dots. They should not be interchanged—a white pin should not be used with a black piston.*

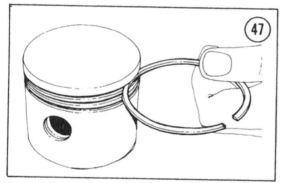

Reassembly

Reassemble the piston and cylinder in reverse order of disassembly.

1. Before reinstalling the pistons on connecting rods, check to see that the piston pin is parallel to the cylinder seating surface on the crankcase. This check should be made with the engine on its side and the connecting rod in a true vertical position. Push the wrist pin into the connecting rod and place 2 equal height gauge blocks on the seating surface (**Figure 45**).

Rotate the crankshaft slowly until the wrist pin just touches the blocks. If the ends of the pins do not make contact at the same time, insert an arbor in the wrist pin hole and carefully bend the connecting rod in the direction of the high side (**Figure 46**).

2. Check for twist in the connecting rod by inclining the rod to one side of the cylinder hole, and rotating the crank to bring the wrist pin in contact with the blocks. Again, if the ends of the pin do not make contact at the same time, insert an arbor in the wrist pin hole and carefully twist the rod in the direction opposite its present state.

3. Before installing the rings on the pistons, roll the rings in the grooves (**Figure 47**) to make sure there are no obstructions in the grooves, and that the clearances are correct.

4. Install the rings, preferably with a ring expander, making sure the manufacturer's marks are toward the top, and the gaps are spaced 120 degrees apart.

5. Attach the pistons to the rods with the VORN, or the arrow, pointing forward (**Figure 48**). This is important because all models other than the R 60 and R 69 have offset wrist pins.

6. Push the pins into the pistons, mating the piston to the connecting rod. It may be necessary to heat the pistons slightly.

7. Install new snap rings so that one end of the ring crosses the removal groove in the piston (**Figure 49**).

8. Before installing the cylinder, recheck to see that the ring gaps are offset by 120 degrees. Install a ring compressor (BMW tool No. 5003) on the piston. Slip the barrel over the head of the piston and tap the barrel in place.

9. Reinstall the head according to the instructions in this chapter.

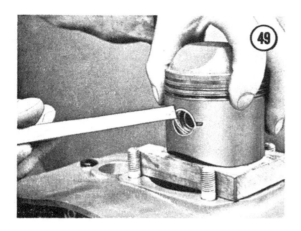

CRANKSHAFT
AND CONNECTING RODS

Removal

The crankshaft assembly (**Figure 50**) has pressed-in rod journals to accomodate the one-piece connecting rods and roller bearings. Between 9,000 and 13,000 pounds of pressure are required to remove and reinstall the crank pins in the web. If any of the conditions and dimensions you will be checking for are not within specifications, it is recommended that the crank and rod assembly be replaced as a unit.

The following steps should be performed in accordance with the instructions in this chapter.

1. Remove the engine from the chassis.

2. Remove the cylinder heads, pistons, and cylinders.

3. Remove the magneto and generator.

4. Remove the clutch and flywheel.

5. Remove the timing gears and the camshaft.

6. Remove the front timing case.

7. Unscrew six 10mm bolts and four 13mm nuts from the front bearing cover plate. Install the puller (BMW tool No. 536), with the 2 bolts screwed into the threaded holes in the bearing cover (**Figure 51**), and remove the cover by turning the puller bolt clockwise.

CAUTION
*Be careful not to damage the oil spray
jet while removing the cover.*

8. Remove the bolts (one on R 50, two on R 60 and R 69) which fasten the oil slinger to the

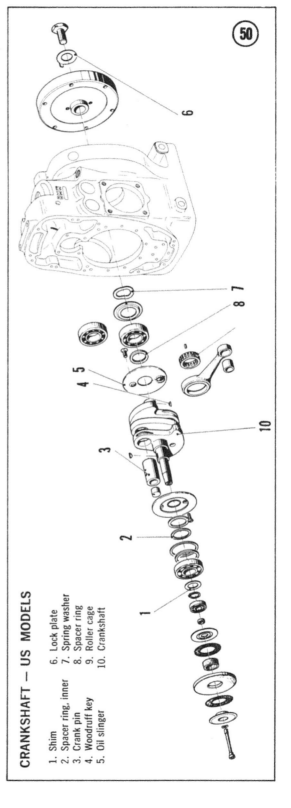

CRANKSHAFT — US MODELS

1. Shim
2. Spacer ring, inner
3. Crank pin
4. Woodruff key
5. Oil slinger
6. Lock plate
7. Spring washer
8. Spacer ring
9. Roller cage
10. Crankshaft

front of the crankshaft and remove the slinger and the spacer.

> NOTE: *On R 69 models, remove the rear oil seal and washers and install the guide ring (BMW tool No. 5048) onto the rear of the shaft with the flywheel mounting bolt* (**Figure 52**).

9. Heat rear of engine housing to about 200°F and pull the crankshaft forward to draw the rear bearing out of its seat.

> NOTE: *On R 69 models, remove the guide ring after the bearing has come free.*

10. Turn the crankshaft so that the front web is up (**Figure 53**).

11. Tilt the front of the crankshaft down and carefully lift crank out of engine (**Figure 54**).

12. Carefully clean out both oil slingers. They also serve as sludge traps, and when they fill up they no longer provide adequate lubrication for the rod bearings.

Inspection

1. Check the crankshaft for out-of-roundness (**Figure 55**). It should not be greater than 0.02mm (0.0008 in.) for either main journal. Also, check the journals for damage. Check the connecting rod big-end bearings for play. It should be negligble. If the crankshaft is not within specifications, replace the assembly.

2. Check the main bearings. They should turn freely and smoothly. Check the bearing races for interference fit on the crank journals. It should be 0.015mm (0.0006 in.).

> NOTE: *When replacing the No. 6207 main bearings, be sure the new bearings have* riveted *cages. Folded cages will unfold in about 4,000 miles in this application. Try to get bearings with 9 or 11 balls in them; they are much stronger than the original bearings.*

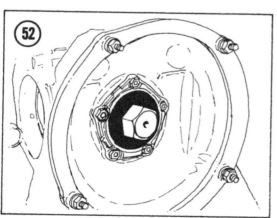

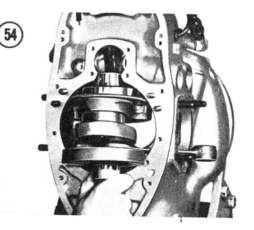

Reassembly

1. Refer to **Figure 56** and reinstall the oil slinger, thin spacer, main bearing, splash ring, and spring washer on the rear of the crankshaft.

2. Heat the engine to 200°F and reinstall the crankshaft into the engine in reverse of the removal procedure. The front web should be turned up with the forward connecting rod on the left and the rear connecting rod on the right. When the crankshaft is in position, push the rear bearing into its seat.

> NOTE: *On R 69 models, install the guide ring (BMW tool No. 5048) on the rear of the crankshaft. This is necessary to set the correct crankshaft end play on this engine.*

3. Reinstall the front oil slinger on the front crankweb (**Figure 57**) and lock the screws by staking them on the edge with a centerpunch.

4. Install the front spacer ring on the crankshaft (**Figure 58**) with the chamfered edge toward the oil slinger.

5. With the crankcase still warm, slip the front bearing retainer onto the crankshaft, making certain the pump casting seats in the front of the crankcase. Install the spindle of the puller (BMW tool No. 355a), with the lever nut (BMW tool No. 535), and the pressure bushing (BMW tool No. 5038/1) onto the bearing in the cover

(**Figure 59**). Screw the spindle of the puller into the end of the crankshaft and pull the bearing onto the crankshaft by turning the lever nut clockwise, until the cover almost touches the crankcase.

> NOTE: *On older models, the cast iron front main bearing retainer is often found to be cracked or broken. The later aluminum front main bearing retainer is fully interchangeable and far stronger. The reason for the problem is that the aluminum crankcase expands faster than the cast iron retainer and the resultant stresses crack the cover. The new aluminum cover has the same coefficient of expansion as the crankcase.*

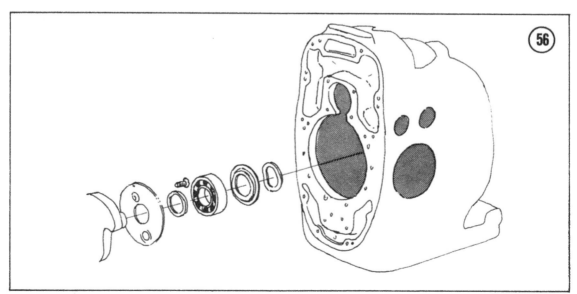

6. Reinstall the 6 bolts (4 long ones at the bottom of the oil pump, 2 shorter ones immediately above) and 4 nuts on the front of the cover, and draw the cover carefully into place by tightening the bolts and nuts in a crosswise pattern.

7. After the cover is secured, continue tightening the lever nut until the shoulder on the crankshaft comes in contact with the bearing inner race.

8. On R 69 models, remove the guide ring tool from the rear of the crankshaft. Install the oil retainer washer with the deep cupped side toward the bearing.

9. Press the oil seal in place with a drift (BMW tool No. 5108) and handle (BMW tool No. 5120) until approximately 1mm (0.039 in.) of the seal protrudes above the surface of the casting around the entire circumference. See **Figure 60**.

CLUTCH AND FLYWHEEL

Disassembly

The clutch and flywheel can be removed with the engine installed in the chassis. In both cases, the transmission must first be removed, and the top and bottom engine mounting bolts must be removed, and the engine pushed forward to permit the transmission to clear.

Removal of the transmission is covered in Chapter Five; this section presents disassembly, inspection, and service of the clutch and flywheel.

1. Remove every other screw from the clutch body with an impact screwdriver (**Figure 61**).

2. Use three 8mm x 1 bolts and 3 matching nuts to relax the clutch spring. Remove every other clutch screw, screw the nuts onto the bolts and run them part way up. Install the bolts into the screw holes, and turn them in about 6 turns. Run the nuts down to the clutch cover plate, and

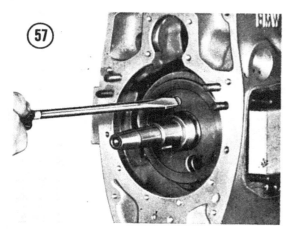

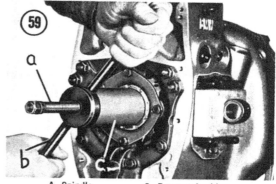

A. Spindle
B. Lever nut
C. Pressure bushing

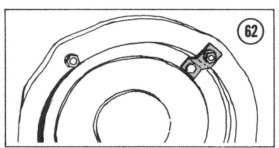

remove the remaining 3 clutch screws. Loosen the nuts off one turn at a time. Reverse this procedure to reassemble. *You must use an impact screwdriver.*

4. Install the flywheel holding fixture (BMW tool No. 292). Straighten the locking edge on the large tab washer, and unscrew the 41mm bolt in the center of the flywheel. If the holding fixture is not available, use a 2 in. long metal plate with two holes drilled in it to lock the flywheel on all models. One hole goes over a transmission mounting stud on the crankcase, and a clutch screw goes through the other hole (**Figure 62**). On all models, you can remove the flywheel bolts with an air wrench without locking the flywheel, but you must lock the flywheel to re-torque the bolts during assembly.

5. Install a puller (BMW tool No. 311, **Figure 63**), and draw the flywheel off the crankshaft by turning the puller bolt clockwise. It may be necessary to rap sharply on the head of the puller bolt while it is being turned.

Inspection

1. With a micrometer, check the thickness of the clutch plate and lining. The combined thickness should be 4.5mm (0.1772 in.) or greater. If it is not, replace it.

2. Check the runout of the clutch plate with a dial indicator (**Figure 64**). The maximum allowable runout is 0.5mm (0.0197 in.). Carefully straighten the plate if necessary.

3. With a straightedge, check the pressure plate for warp (**Figure 65**), and carefully straighten it if necessary.

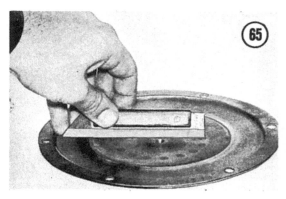

4. Reassemble the clutch, using the centering arbor (BMW tool No. 529, **Figure 66**), and check the diaphragm spring pressure.

> NOTE: *If you suspect the clutch diaphragm spring has lost noticeable tension, have it measured (installed on the flywheel) by a machine shop. Specified diaphragm spring pressures are given in* **Table 8**.

Table 8   CLUTCH DIAPHRAGM
SPRING PRESSURE

Model	Pounds	Kilograms
R 50	330 to 364	150 to 165
R 60. R 69	336 to 397	166 to 180

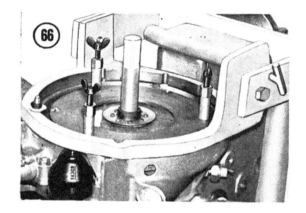

Reassembly

1. Before setting the flywheel in place, check to be sure the spring washer is in place, behind the rear bearing cover (**Figure 67**). Coat the end of the flywheel collar with Molykote. Make sure the Woodruff key is correctly installed in the crankshaft; its flat surface should be parallel to the centerline of the crankshaft.

2. Set the flywheel in place, taking care to line up the Woodruff key with the slot in the flywheel. Coat the inner surface of the head of the flywheel mounting bolt with assembly lube, place the tab washer on the flywheel, and screw in the bolt. Torque bolt to 22-24 mkg (160-175 ft.-lb.). See **Figure 68**.

3. Bend up one edge of the tab washer against a flat on the bolt head (**Figure 69**), to lock the bolt in place.

4. Check the flywheel runout with a dial indicator (**Figure 70**) by slowly rotating the flywheel 360 degrees while observing the indicator. Maximum allowable runout is 0.10mm (0.004 in.). If it exceeds this, and the flywheel is correctly seated, it should be straightened by a professional machine shop.

5. Reinstall the clutch in the reverse order of disassembly, using the centering arbor (BMW tool No. 529, **Figure 71**). Torque the mounting screw to 1.5-2.0 mkg (10.8-14.5 ft.-lb.).

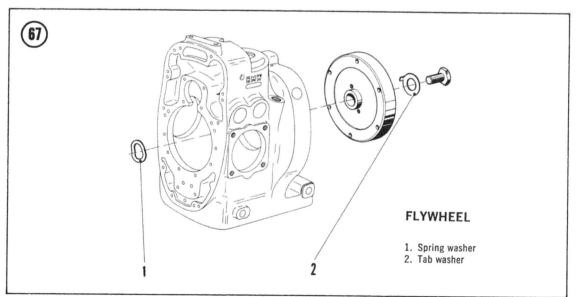

FLYWHEEL

1. Spring washer
2. Tab washer

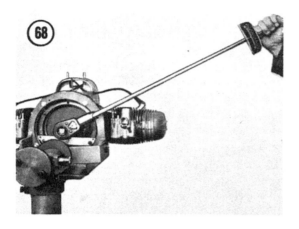

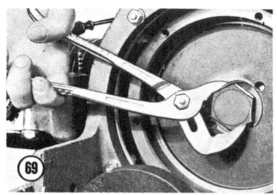

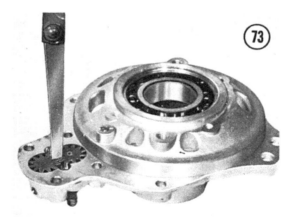

OIL PUMP

The oil pump is a gear type, driven off the front of the crankshaft by spur gears. The pump draws oil from the sump, through an oil strainer, and supplies it to the engine under pressure. Servicing of the oil sump and strainer are covered in Chapter Three.

Disassembly

1. Remove the engine from the chassis.

2. Remove the magneto and generator.

3. Remove the timing gears, the timing case, front crankshaft bearings, and the drive gear.

4. Unscrew the six 10mm bolts, and four 13mm

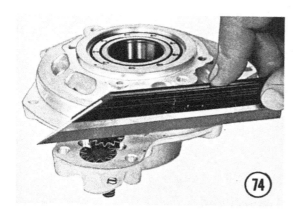

nuts from the front bearing cover plate. Install
a puller (BMW tool No. 536), with 2 bolts
screwed into the threaded holes in the bearing
cover (**Figure 72**), and remove the cover by
turning the puller bolt clockwise.

Inspection

1. Measure the backlash between the oil pump
gears with a feeler gauge (**Figure 73**). It should
be between 0.1-0.25mm (0.0039-0.0098 in.). If
the backlash is excessive, replace the gearset.

2. Measure the side play of the gears, in the
cover plate, with a straightedge (**Figure 74**). The
play should be between 0.010 and 0.04mm
(0.0004 and 0.0016 in.). If the side play is excessive, replace the gearset.

Reassembly

To reinstall the oil pump and reassemble the
timing and ignition systems, refer to the reassembly procedure for the crankshaft, beginning
with Step 5, in this chapter.

CHAPTER FIVE

TRANSMISSION

The transmission is a 4-speed constant-mesh unit. See **Figure 1**.

Figure 2 shows the power flow through the transmission for each gear.

Removal

1. Put the motorcycle on its centerstand and place a jackstand beneath the frame in line with the swinging arm pivot (**Figure 3**).

2. Disconnect the battery leads (ground first) and remove the battery and the battery holder.

3. Remove the carburetor intake tubes and the carburetor from the left cylinder, the air filter housing, and the air filter (**Figure 4**).

4. Unscrew the speedometer drive retaining bolt (**Figure 5**), and disconnect the cable.

5. Remove the hose clamp from the dust boot over the universal joint (**Figure 6**) and push the boot back as far as it will go.

6. Unscrew the 4 retaining bolts from the universal joint (**Figure 7**).

7. Remove the footbrake pivot bolt and disconnect the clutch actuating cable from the throwout lever, and ground strap, and the neutral indicator wire. Remove the throwout lever from the transmission (**Figure 8**).

8. Unscrew the 4 transmission mounting bolts (**Figure 9**).

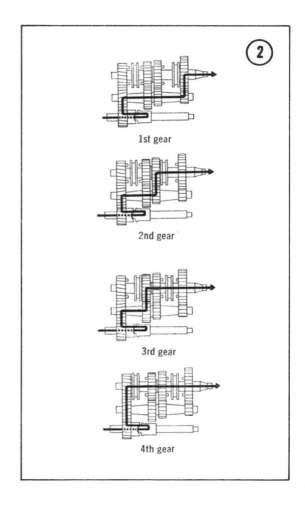

1st gear

2nd gear

3rd gear

4th gear

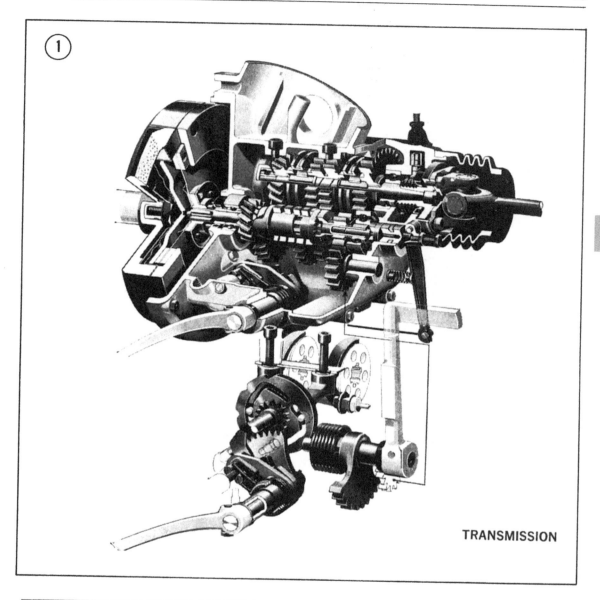

TRANSMISSION

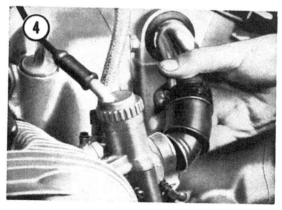

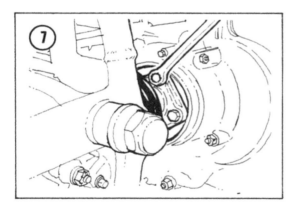

1. Neutral indicator wire   3. Throwout lever
2. Ground strap

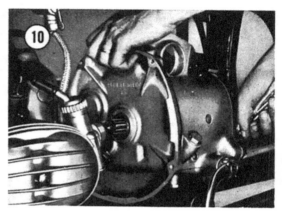

9. Remove the rear wheel. Refer to Chapter Eleven (*Final Drive*) and remove the rear drive housing. Unbolt the upper mount on the left shock absorber.

10. Support the swinging arm in a horizontal position.

11. Remove the rubber boot from the drive shaft housing. Pull the drive shaft back into the housing as far as it will go.

12. Pull the transmission back from the engine to disengage the input shaft from the flywheel and remove it to the left (**Figure 10**).

NOTE: *When removing the transmission with the rear swinging arm installed, remove the top and bottom mounting bolts, and push the engine as far forward as it will go before removing transmission.*

Output Flange Seal Replacement

Figures 11 and 12 are presented as general refernces for removal and replacement of the output flange and its seal.

1. Mount the transmission in the workstand (BMW tool No. 6000) with the adapter (BMW tool No. 6005, **Figure 13**).

2. Remove the drain screw and drain the transmission oil.

3. Remove the cotter key from the clutch lever pin (**Figure 14**) and remove the pin and lever.

4. Install the fixture (BMW tool No. 500) on the coupling flange and unscrew the grooved nut on the end of the transmission shaft with a socket (BMW tool No. 494/3, **Figure 15**).

5. Fasten a Matra 501 puller to the coupling flange and pull the flange off by turning the puller bolt clockwise (**Figure 16**). It may be necessary to rap lightly on the head of the puller bolt as it is turned.

6. The speedometer worm gear and its bushing may be left in place if they are not worn. If they are to be removed, however, unscrew the 8mm bolt, and lever the bushing and gear out of the boss with 2 screwdrivers set against the edge of the bushing flange.

7. Remove the output shaft oil seal, and inspect it for wear or damage. If it is worn, replace it with a new seal, installing it with the sealing lip facing the rear of the housing cover, and permitting about 1mm (0.039 in.) of the seal to protrude above the housing cover.

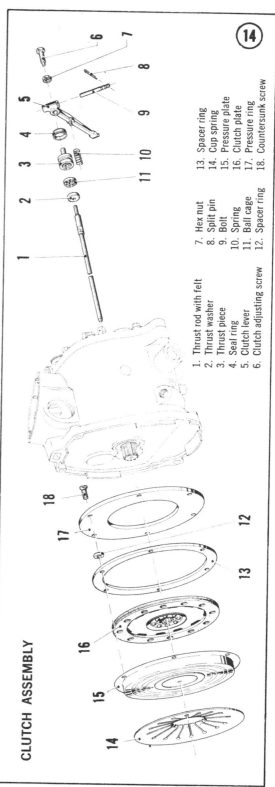

CLUTCH ASSEMBLY

1. Thrust rod with felt
2. Thrust washer
3. Thrust piece
4. Seal ring
5. Clutch lever
6. Clutch adjusting screw
7. Hex nut
8. Split pin
9. Bolt
10. Spring
11. Ball cage
12. Spacer ring
13. Spacer ring
14. Cup spring
15. Pressure plate
16. Clutch plate
17. Pressure ring
18. Countersunk screw

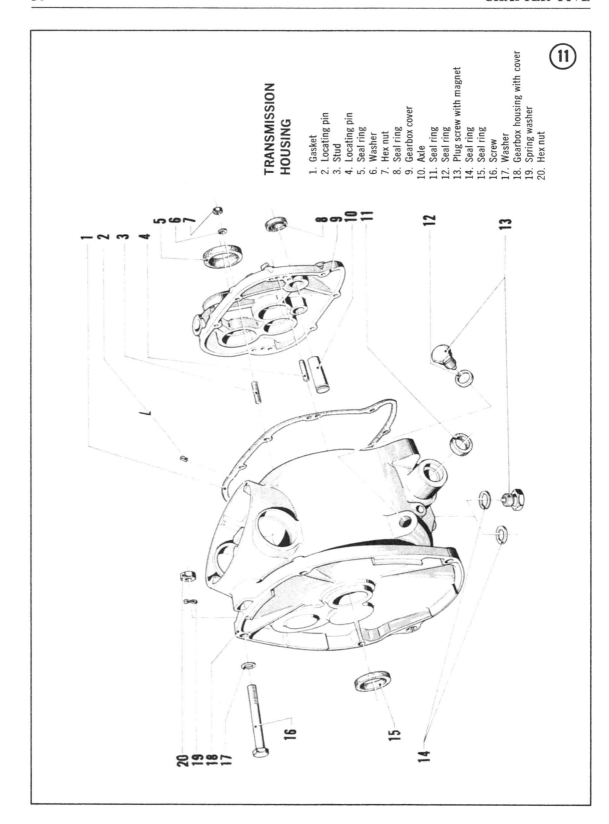

TRANSMISSION HOUSING

1. Gasket
2. Locating pin
3. Stud
4. Locating pin
5. Seal ring
6. Washer
7. Hex nut
8. Seal ring
9. Gearbox cover
10. Axle
11. Seal ring
12. Seal ring
13. Plug screw with magnet
14. Seal ring
15. Seal ring
16. Screw
17. Washer
18. Gearbox housing with cover
19. Spring washer
20. Hex nut

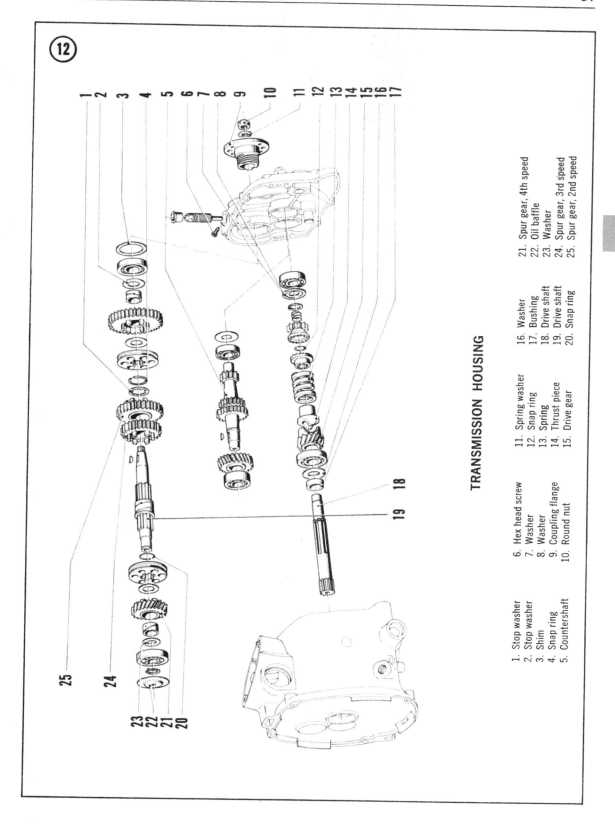

TRANSMISSION HOUSING

1. Stop washer
2. Stop washer
3. Shim
4. Snap ring
5. Countershaft

6. Hex head screw
7. Washer
8. Washer
9. Coupling flange
10. Round nut

11. Spring washer
12. Snap ring
13. Spring
14. Thrust piece
15. Drive gear

16. Washer
17. Bushing
18. Drive shaft
19. Drive shaft
20. Snap ring

21. Spur gear, 4th speed
22. Oil baffle
23. Washer
24. Spur gear, 3rd speed
25. Spur gear, 2nd speed

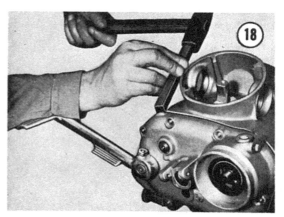

Transmission Shaft Removal

1. Remove the output flange and seal, and remove the complete clutch throwout mechanism, including the rod (**Figure 14**).

2. Remove the seven 10mm nuts and their washers (**Figure 17**).

3. Heat transmission housing to about 180°F, press the kickstarter down, and then tap the cover off, using a hard wood stick held against the removal knobs on the cover (**Figure 18**).

> NOTE: *Push the washer (part No. 7,* **Figure 12**) *to the rear with a long, thin screwdriver as you remove the rear cover. It usually does not slide off the shaft as you withdraw the cover, but cocks and jams the cover halfway off. Use finesse, not force.*

4. Remove the end play shims from the cover.

5. Mark the shifting forks and their respective eccentric bushings for position.

6. Refer to **Figure 19** and unscrew the two 6mm Allen bolts which hold the shifting forks (**Figure 20**). Remove the retaining plate.

7. With the housing still warm, remove the 3 transmission shafts, along with the shifting forks, as a unit (**Figure 21**). It may be necessary to tap on the housing with a soft-face mallet to free the shafts from their bearings. Make sure the shifting forks clear the opening in the case. Remove the oil baffle from the output shaft bearing seat in the housing.

Input Shaft Disassembly

1. Remove the thrust washer, spring, and kickstarter gear (**Figure 22**).

2. Compress the shock absorber spring (BMW tool No. 319/1) and remove circlip (**Figure 23**).

3. Remove the kickstarter ratchet, the kickstarter spring, the drive coupling, and the drive gear from the input shaft (**Figure 24**). It is not

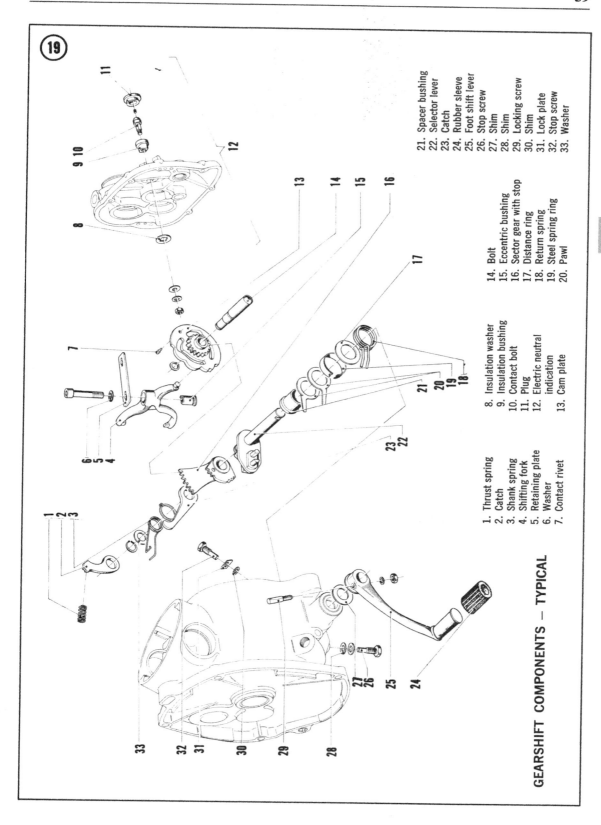

(19)

1. Thrust spring
2. Catch
3. Shank spring
4. Shifting fork
5. Retaining plate
6. Washer
7. Contact rivet
8. Insulation washer
9. Insulation bushing
10. Contact bolt
11. Plug
12. Electric neutral indication
13. Cam plate
14. Bolt
15. Eccentric bushing
16. Sector gear with stop
17. Distance ring
18. Return spring
19. Steel spring ring
20. Pawl
21. Spacer bushing
22. Selector lever
23. Catch
24. Rubber sleeve
25. Foot shift lever
26. Stop screw
27. Shim
28. Shim
29. Locking screw
30. Shim
31. Lock plate
32. Stop screw
33. Washer

GEARSHIFT COMPONENTS — TYPICAL

necessary to remove the ball bearing assembly, the washer, and the sleeve unless they are damaged or worn and require replacement.

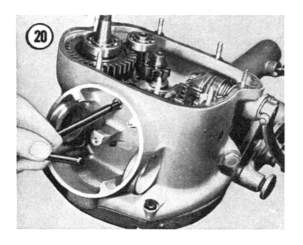

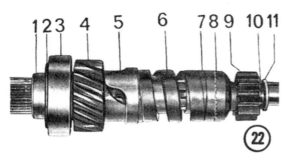

1. Bushing
2. Washer
3. Ball bearing
4. Gear
5. Drive coupling
6. Spring
7. Kickstarter coupling
8. Kickstarter coupling
9. Intermediate gear
10. Spring
11. Thrust washer

Output Shaft Disassembly

1. Place the output shaft in a press tube, with first gear supported by split plates (**Figure 25**). Press off the gear, the thrust washer, and the ball bearing.

2. Refer to **Figure 26** and remove the floating bushing, the second washer, and the sliding coupling for first and second gear. Remove the circlip and splined washer, and then second and third gear.

3. Remove the circlip from the forward end of the output shaft and place 2 bars between fourth gear and the sliding coupling. Set the shaft in a press tube (**Figure 27**) and press off the bearing. Then, remove the float bushing, the washers, and sliding coupling.

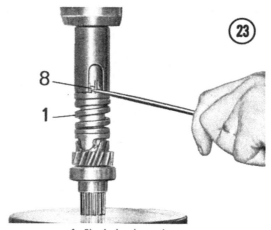

1. Shock absorber spring
8. Circlip

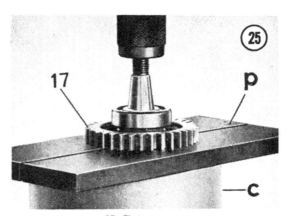

17. First gear
c. Press tube
p. Split plate

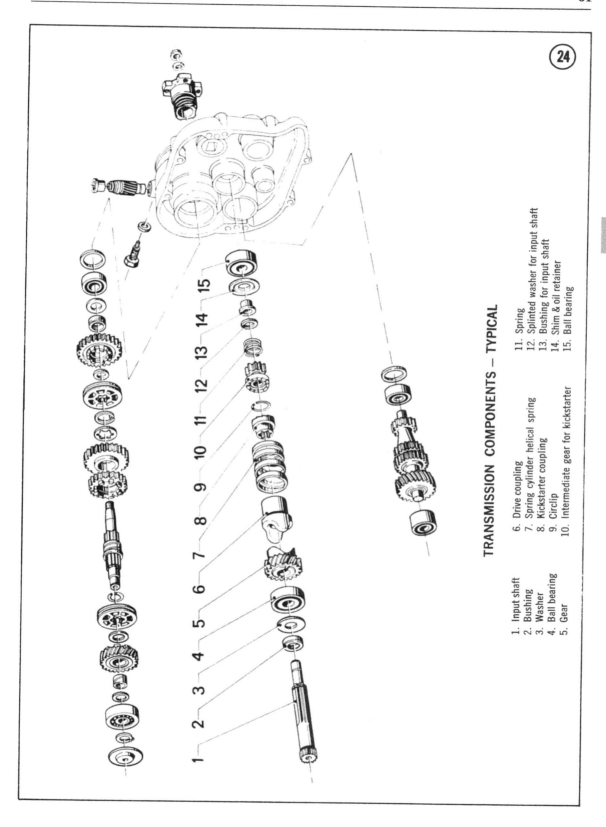

TRANSMISSION COMPONENTS – TYPICAL

1. Input shaft
2. Bushing
3. Washer
4. Ball bearing
5. Gear

6. Drive coupling
7. Spring cylinder helical spring
8. Kickstarter coupling
9. Circlip
10. Intermediate gear for kickstarter

11. Spring
12. Splinted washer for input shaft
13. Bushing for input shaft
14. Shim & oil retainer
15. Ball bearing

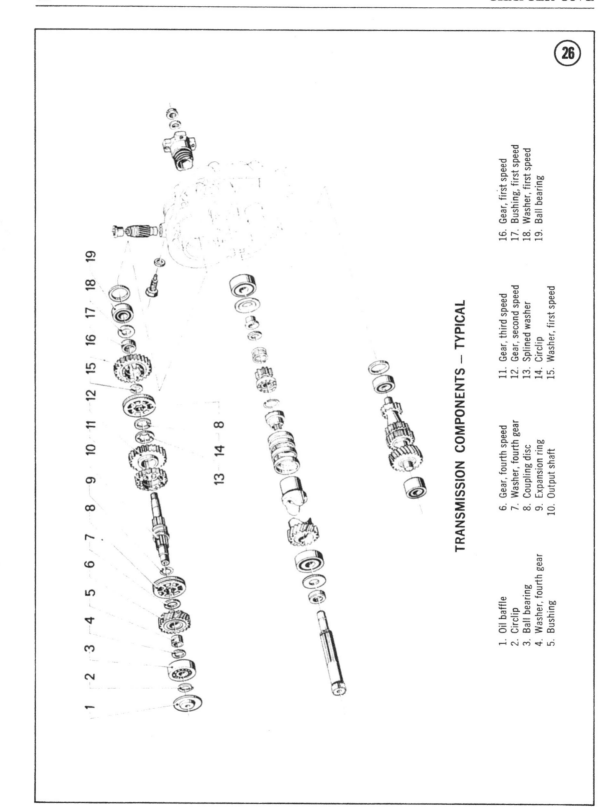

(26)

TRANSMISSION COMPONENTS — TYPICAL

1. Oil baffle
2. Circlip
3. Ball bearing
4. Washer, fourth gear
5. Bushing

6. Gear, fourth speed
7. Washer, fourth gear
8. Coupling disc
9. Expansion ring
10. Output shaft

11. Gear, third speed
12. Gear, second speed
13. Splined washer
14. Circlip
15. Washer, first speed

16. Gear, first speed
17. Bushing, first speed
18. Washer, first speed
19. Ball bearing

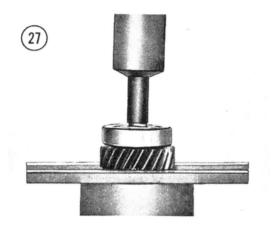

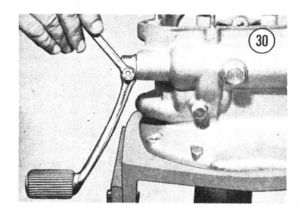

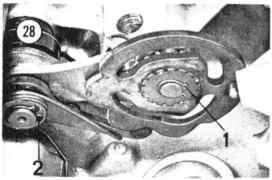

1. Circlip (cam plate)   2. Circlip (detent spring)

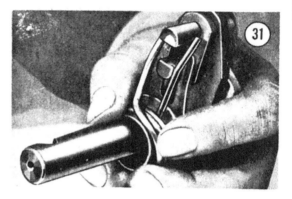

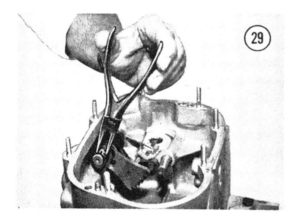

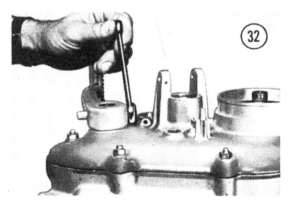

3. Remove the nut and bolt from the gear selector (**Figure 30**), and remove the selector and spacer.

4. Remove the entire shift selector assembly (**Figure 31**).

Kickstarter Removal

1. Unscrew the nut from the wedge bolt, tap out the bolt, and remove the kickstarter from the shaft (**Figure 32**).

Selector Mechanism Removal

1. Remove the circlip and shift cam plate (**Figure 28**), and then remove the second circlip and washer and detent spring.

2. Remove the circlip, pawl, and shift segment (**Figure 29**).

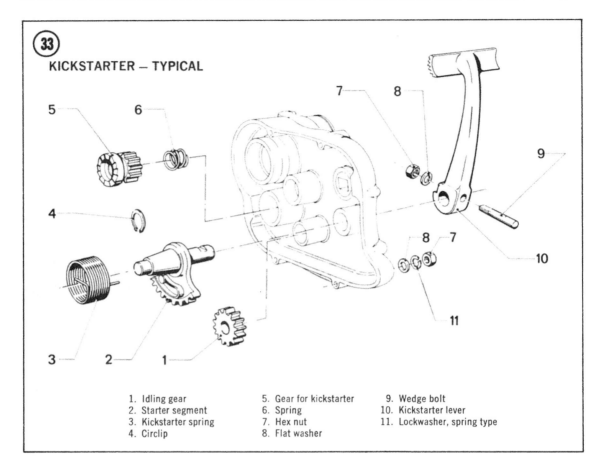

33

KICKSTARTER – TYPICAL

1. Idling gear	5. Gear for kickstarter	9. Wedge bolt
2. Starter segment	6. Spring	10. Kickstarter lever
3. Kickstarter spring	7. Hex nut	11. Lockwasher, spring type
4. Circlip	8. Flat washer	

2. Refer to **Figure 33** and remove the quadrant and return spring from the cover. Remove the circlip from idler shaft and remove idler gear.

Transmission Inspection

1. Check all gears, bearings, bushings, shafts, and spacers for wear, galling, pitting, and chipped and broken teeth and splines. Replace those pieces that are not in good condition.

2. Check the play between the gears and bushings. Measure the gear bores with an inside micrometer, and the bushings with an outside micrometer. Subtract the bushing dimension from the gear dimension to determine the play. If the clearances exceed the specifications (**Table 1**), replace the bushings.

3. Check the play between the bushings and the shafts, with inside and outside micrometers. If the clearances exceed specifications (**Table 2**), replace the bushings.

Table 1   GEAR-TO-BUSHING CLEARANCES

Gear	Clearance
1st and 3rd	0.04-0.09mm (0.0016-0.0035 in.)
2nd and 4th	0.02-0.06mm (0.0008-0.0024 in.)

Table 2   SHAFT-TO-BUSHING CLEARANCES

Gear	Clearance
1st	0.009-0.031mm (0.0004-0.0012 in.)
2nd and 3rd*	0.005-0.047mm (0.0002-0.0019 in.)

*Early models have prefitted bushings and shafts which must be replaced together. Later models have replaceable bushings. Check with your dealer when ordering replacement parts.

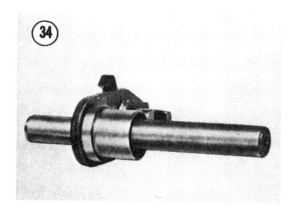

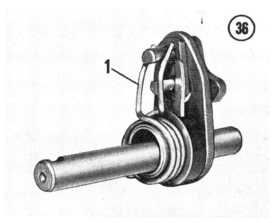

1. Return spring

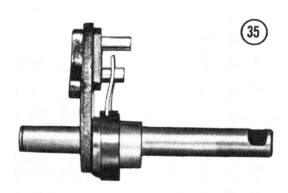

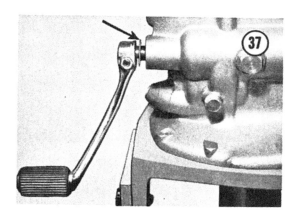

Shim (arrow)

Transmission Reassembly

Reassemble the transmission in reverse order of the disassembly.

1. Install the bushing on the gear selector assembly with the shoulder of the bushing toward the inner lever (**Figure 34**).

2. Insert the positioners in the circular leaf spring and slide the assembly over the bushing, with one positioner on each side of the shorter pin (**Figure 35**).

3. Install the washer, and then the return spring (**Figure 36**), with the curved ends of the spring toward the lever.

4. Install the complete assembly into the transmission housing. The return spring ends must straddle the pin in the housing.

5. Replace shim on selector shaft and reinstall selector lever and wedge bolt. Check end play of shaft (**Figure 37**). It should be 0.2mm (0.0079 in.). If it is not, correct it with another shim of different thickness.

6. Slide the segment and selector gear onto the shaft. The engagement notches in the selector lever must be equal distance from the selecting teeth on both sides of the segment. It may be necessary to bend the return spring to correctly position the selector lever (**Figure 38**).

7. Install the pawl on the segment and secure it with a circlip. Install the detent spring and washer and secure them with the other circlip.

8. Install the shift cam plate. The second tooth on the segment must mesh with the marked tooth on the cam plate (**Figure 39**). Install the circlip.

9. Check the overshift between the pawl and detent notches (**Figure 40**). The overshift should be 1mm (0.039 in.). If it is not, correct it with a shim on the selector limiting bolt.

10. Reinstall kickstarter idler gear and circlip.

11. If the kickstarter spring has been removed from the quadrant, place the vertical tip of the spring over the gear, and with the help of a screwdriver and a pair of pliers (**Figure 41**), wind the spring clockwise until its upper end can be inserted into the hole in the quadrant shaft.

12. Install the starter quadrant in the cover. Use a pair of pliers to guide the end of the spring into the hole in the cover (**Figure 42**).

13. Refer to **Figure 26** and reassemble the output shaft.

14. Refer to **Figure 24** for assembly of the input shaft. If the front bushing, washer, and ball bearing assembly have been removed, press them back on.

15. Install the drive gear, the torsion damper coupling, spring, and ratchet (**Figure 43**). Place the tapered sleeve (BMW tool No. 319/1) over the end of the shaft, with the taper up, and slide the circlip down the taper as far as it will go. Place the installer (BMW tool No. 319/2) over the taper, and with a vise or press, press the damper together until the circlip snaps into its groove.

16. Install the kickstarter gear, ratchet spring, and a new thrust washer; this is important because the washer must be snug on the shaft so it will not be pushed off by the ratchet spring.

17. If the output shaft, the couplings, or the forks have been replaced with new ones, the forks must be readjusted. Heat the transmission housing to 180-210°F and install the fixture (BMW tool No. 504). See **Figure 44**.

18. Install the shifting forks into the sliding couplings, and into the shift cam plate. Then, secure the forks with the 2 Allen bolts.

> NOTE: *The bolt can be installed easily if the cam plate is placed in the fourth gear position for installation of the bolt on the third/forth gear fork, and in the second gear position for installation of the bolt in the first/second gear fork.*

19. Move the cam to neutral. Adjust the forks by rotating the eccentric bushings until the sliding couplings are centered exactly between their

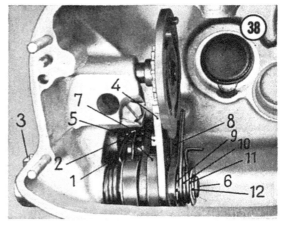

1. Spring ends	7. Interlock pawl
2. Jam pilot pin	8. Ratchet plate
3. Shift lever	9. Snap ring
4. Sector gear	10. Ratchet plate
5. Interlock gear	11. Washer
6. Lever shaft	12. Spring

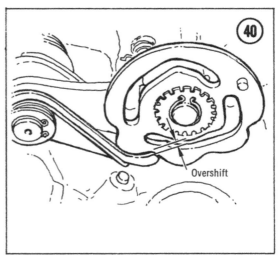

Overshift

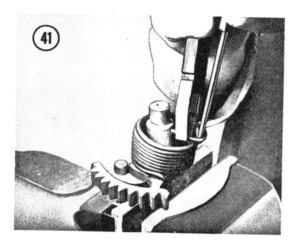

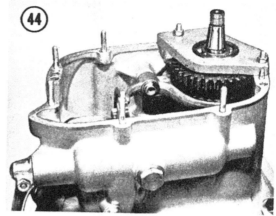

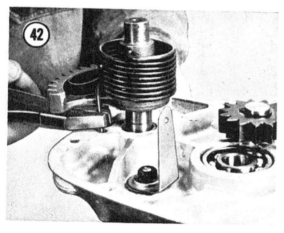

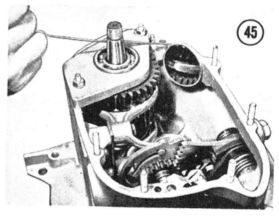

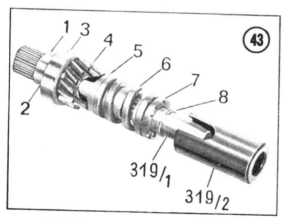

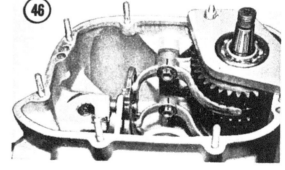

1. Seal sleeve
2. Washer
3. Ball bearing
4. Input shaft
5. Drive coupling
6. Kickstarter spring
7. Kickstarter ratchet
8. Circlip
319/1 BMW tool
319/2 BMW tool

respective gears. Use an inspection mirror for this (**Figure 45**).

20. Make sure that the ears on the forks are fully engaged in the couplings, and that the couplings are not pressed against the gears.

21. Mark the position of each eccentric bushing on its shifting fork (**Figure 46**), and remove the output shaft and forks from the transmission.

22. If necessary, reheat the transmission housing to 180-210°F. Insert the input shaft assembly into its bore in the transmission, place the sleeve (BMW tool No. 206) over the shaft (**Figure 47**), and tap the shaft into place.

CAUTION
Never hammer directly on the end of the shaft.

23. Place the oil guide for the output shaft into the bearing bore.

24. Insert the output shaft, the cluster gear, and the shift forks, as a unit, into the transmission (**Figure 48**). Make sure the shift forks do not bind on the edges of the case opening.

25. Place a new gasket on the transmission housing and then install the fixture (BMW tool No. 504) to support end of output shaft (**Figure 49**). Measure the distance from the upper edge of the ball bearing to the surface of gasket.

26. Measure the distance from the mating surface of the cover to the bottom of the bearing bore (**Figure 50**). Subtract the previous dimension from this one to determine the actual end play. Shim the difference to 0.1mm (0.0039 in.) end play. Prior to installing the cover, hold the shims in place with a small bit of grease.

27. Measure the end play of the cluster shaft in exactly the same manner. Its end play also should be 0.1mm (0.0039 in.).

28. Place a 20mm (0.787 in.) bushing (BMW tool No. 5061) on the end of the input shaft and measure the distance from the top surface of the bushing to the mating surface of the transmission housing (**Figure 51**). Subtract 20mm (0.787 in.)—the thickness of the bushing—from the measurement.

29. Next, measure the distance from the mating surface of the cover to the shoulder of the bushing, installed in the bearing (**Figure 52**). Subtract the result from the previous measurement and shim the difference to 0.1mm (0.0039 in.) with a shim/oil retainer.

30. Remove the bushing from the bearing (**Figure 53**) and place the correct retainer on the bearing, with its raised outer edge facing the transmission. Then, reinstall the bushing.

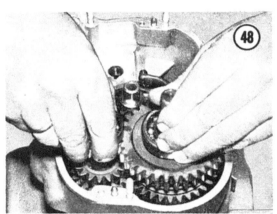

31. Check the position of the neutral indicator contact with a gauge (BMW tool No. 5097, **Figure 54**). If necessary, bend or file the contact carefully until it just touches the gauge.

NOTE: *Stick the cupped spacer (part No. 7, **Figure 12**) to the input shaft bearing in the rear cover with stiff grease. The edges of the spacer should stick up and the center should be flush with the inside bore of the bearing.*

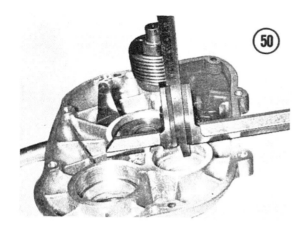

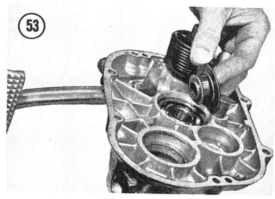

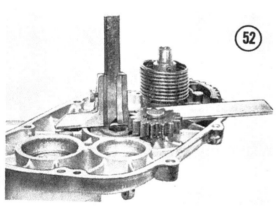

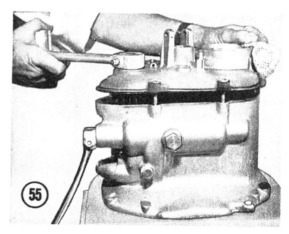

32. Heat the cover to 180-210°F, start it onto the shaft, and depress the kickstarter part way (**Figure 55**). Slowly, push the cover into place, and at the same time carefully move the starter lever up and down until its engagement with the starter gear can be felt. Then, tap the cover all the way down and install the nuts, tightening them in a crosswise pattern.

33. Double check the operation of the neutral indicator by attaching the negative terminal of the battery to the transmission, and connecting a continuity light between the positive battery terminal and the neural indicator connector on the transmission. With the transmission in neutral, the light should be on, and when it is shifted into first or second gear the light should go out.

CHAPTER SIX

FUEL SYSTEM

CARBURETORS

The carburetors used on BMW twins are a conventional slide, side-mounted, float bowl type (**Figure 1**).

Adjustment procedures are presented in Chapter Three. This chapter outlines disassembly and inspection.

Disassembly

The parts of the carburetor are shown in **Figures 2 and 3**. Refer to these figures while performing the following steps.

1. Refer to Chapter Three and remove the carburetors from the engine.

2. Carefully dismantle the carburetors, making sure not to mix the parts.

3. Remove the jets and place them in individually labeled envelopes.

Inspection and Adjustment

1. See Chapter Three and check float level.

2. Check the float valve for wear. If either the needle or seat are worn, replace them.

3. Clean each jet with compressed air. Do not use wire to poke dirt from the jets. Hard steel wire can create burrs in the soft brass jets, altering their flow rates. If compressed air alone will

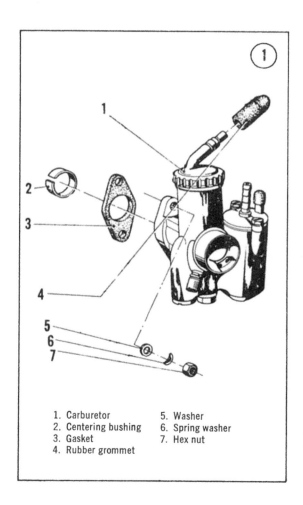

1. Carburetor
2. Centering bushing
3. Gasket
4. Rubber grommet
5. Washer
6. Spring washer
7. Hex nut

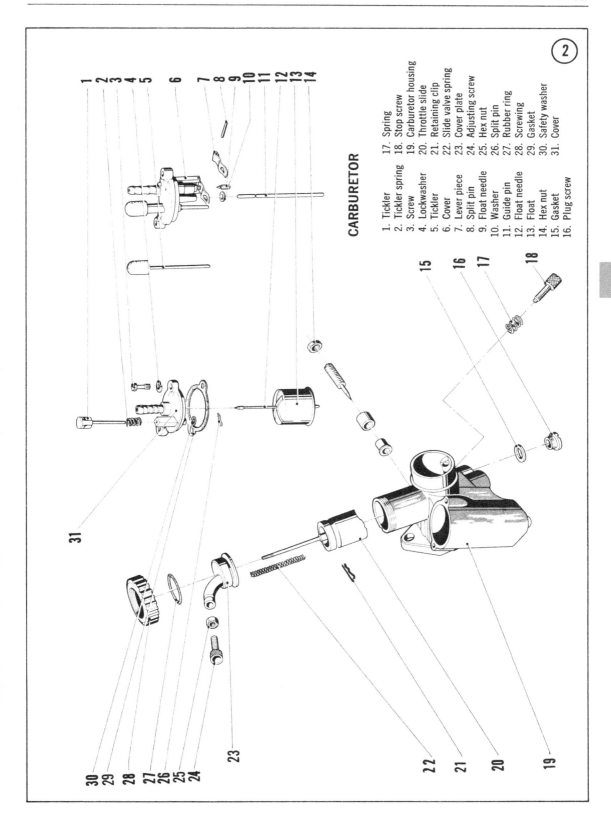

CARBURETOR

1. Tickler
2. Tickler spring
3. Screw
4. Lockwasher
5. Tickler
6. Cover
7. Lever piece
8. Split pin
9. Float needle
10. Washer
11. Guide pin
12. Float needle
13. Float
14. Hex nut
15. Gasket
16. Plug screw
17. Spring
18. Stop screw
19. Carburetor housing
20. Throttle slide
21. Retaining clip
22. Slide valve spring
23. Cover plate
24. Adjusting screw
25. Hex nut
26. Split pin
27. Rubber ring
28. Screwing
29. Gasket
30. Safety washer
31. Cover

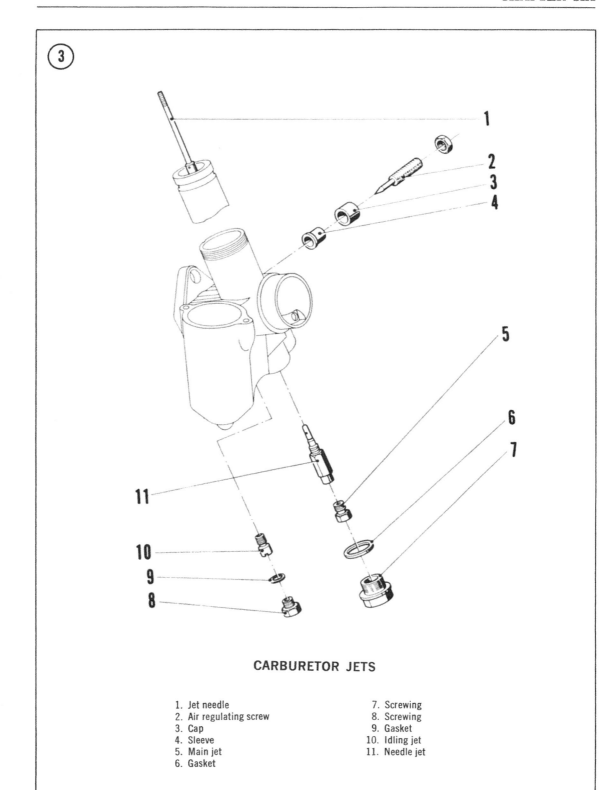

CARBURETOR JETS

1. Jet needle
2. Air regulating screw
3. Cap
4. Sleeve
5. Main jet
6. Gasket
7. Screwing
8. Screwing
9. Gasket
10. Idling jet
11. Needle jet

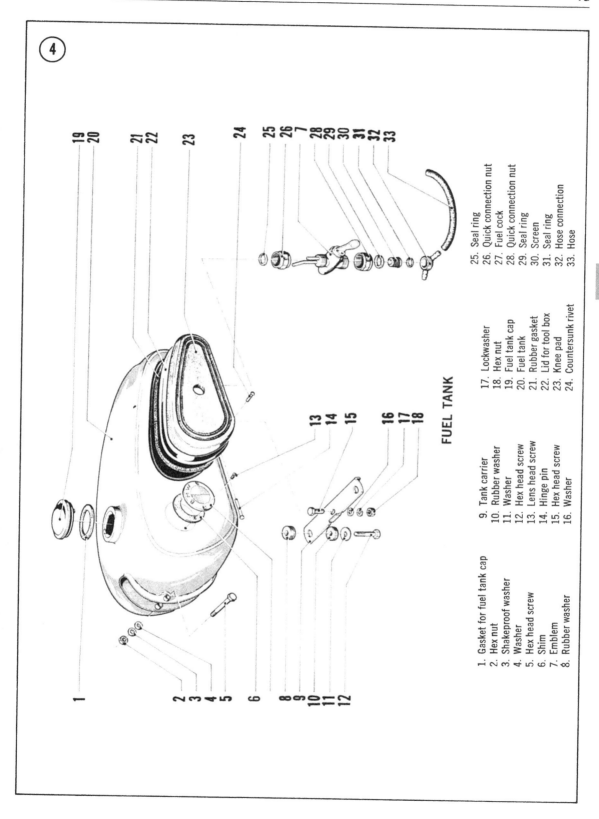

FUEL TANK

1. Gasket for fuel tank cap
2. Hex nut
3. Shakeproof washer
4. Washer
5. Hex head screw
6. Shim
7. Emblem
8. Rubber washer
9. Tank carrier
10. Rubber washer
11. Washer
12. Hex head screw
13. Lens head screw
14. Hinge pin
15. Hex head screw
16. Washer
17. Lockwasher
18. Hex nut
19. Fuel tank cap
20. Fuel tank
21. Rubber gasket
22. Lid for tool box
23. Knee pad
24. Countersunk rivet
25. Seal ring
26. Quick connection nut
27. Fuel cock
28. Quick connection nut
29. Seal ring
30. Screen
31. Seal ring
32. Hose connection
33. Hose

not remove an obstruction, use a broomstraw.

4. Check gaskets and sealing washers to see if they are damaged or excessively compressed. Replace them if necessary.

FUEL TANK AND FUEL VALVE

Figure 4 is an exploded view of the fuel tank and fuel valve.

Disassembly

1. Turn off the fuel valve and pull the fuel lines off the T-connector.

2. Remove the seat.

3. Remove the mounting bolt at the front of the fuel tank. Remove the 2 rubber-bushed bolts, beneath the tank on each side, that fasten the tank to the carrier bar. Then, lift off the tank.

4. Empty the fuel tank and remove the fuel valve by unscrewing large union nut at the top.

> NOTE: *The tank should not remain empty for long periods, otherwise the sealing gaskets will dry out and leak.*

5. Disassemble the fuel valve (**Figure 5**).

> NOTE: *The narrow shoulder ends of the 2 unions have left-hand threads.*

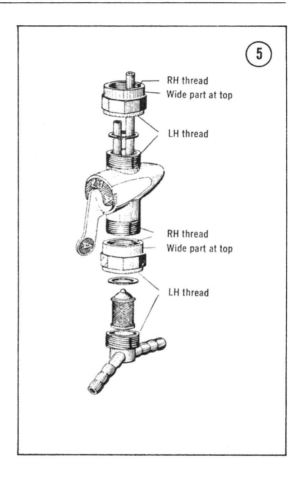

(5)

RH thread
Wide part at top

LH thread

RH thread
Wide part at top

LH thread

CHAPTER SEVEN

IGNITION AND CHARGING SYSTEMS

Ignition systems, charging systems, and batteries are presented in this chapter. Routine adjustments for the ignition systems are covered in Chapter Three.

IGNITION

BMW's are equipped with magneto ignition with automatic spark advance control (**Figure 1**). The magneto rotor is driven directly off the end of the camshaft, at one-half engine speed. The magneto consists of a permanent magnet (the rotor), a fixed stator combined with a coil, a contact breaker, and an automatic advance mechanism (**Figure 2**).

The firing point (static timing) occurs 9 degrees BTC. The timing range covers 30 degrees, with maximum advance occurring at 39 ± 2 degrees BTC.

> NOTE: *Before beginning work on the magneto, remove your watch, if you are wearing one, to prevent it from becoming magnetized.*

Disassembly

1. Remove the front engine cover.
2. Remove the Allen screw from the advance mechanism (**Figure 3**) and carefully pull it off.
3. Remove the contact breaker and condenser.

4. Disconnect the 2 high-tension leads from the ignition coil terminals. Then, unscrew the retaining nuts on either side of the magneto body and remove it.
5. Remove the rotor from the end of the camshaft with a puller (BMW tool No. 5030). See **Figure 4**.

Inspection

Inspection procedures, reassembly steps, and adjustment are covered in Chapter Three.

Coil Testing

The ignition coils should be tested with an electrical bench tester. If you have such a tester,

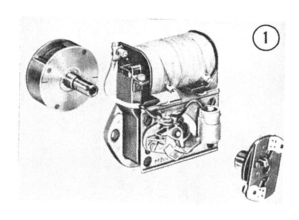

follow the instructions included with it and check the spark length. At start (300 sparks per minute) the spark length should be 8mm (0.3120 in.). At engine operating speeds (3,600 sparks per minute) spark length should be 13.5mm (0.532 in.).

If you do not have access to a bench tester,

have the coil checked by an automotive or motorcycle electrical service specialist.

Reassembly

1. Remount the coils with the Allen bolts. Be sure the ground wire is connected to the front bolt on the left coil. Reconnect the input wires

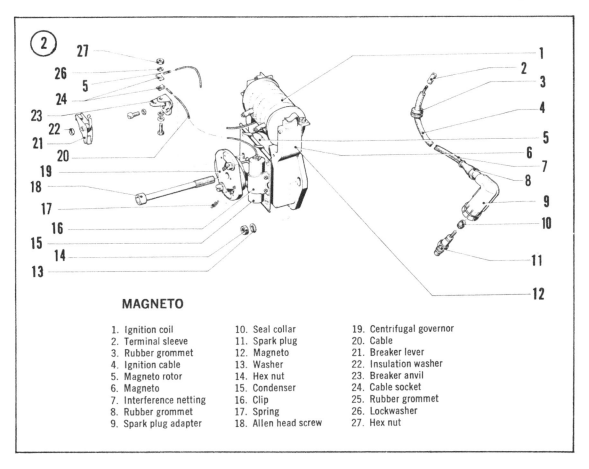

MAGNETO

1. Ignition coil	10. Seal collar	19. Centrifugal governor
2. Terminal sleeve	11. Spark plug	20. Cable
3. Rubber grommet	12. Magneto	21. Breaker lever
4. Ignition cable	13. Washer	22. Insulation washer
5. Magneto rotor	14. Hex nut	23. Breaker anvil
6. Magneto	15. Condenser	24. Cable socket
7. Interference netting	16. Clip	25. Rubber grommet
8. Rubber grommet	17. Spring	26. Lockwasher
9. Spark plug adapter	18. Allen head screw	27. Hex nut

and the high-tension leads.

2. Install the fuel tank. Be careful not to crimp or smash the electrical leads.

Contact Breaker and Advance Mechanisms

Disassembly, inspection, service, and replacement of contact breakers, condensers, and advance mechanisms are covered in Chapter Three.

CHARGING SYSTEM

Generator

There are 3 generator models used. The 6-volt, 60-watt unit (**Figure 5**) is used on most models in this series. An optional 6-volt, 75-watt unit and a 12-volt, 100-watt unit (**Figure 6**) are used on some R 50 S, R 50-2, R 60-2, and R 69 S models. With the exception of its performance, the 75-watt unit is the same as the 60-watt unit.

Some very late models have an optional 3-phase alternator. This unit is discussed later. Determine which unit your motorcycle has and proceed accordingly.

The generator is driven off the end of the crankshaft. It produces its rated output at an engine speed of 1,700 rpm, and its peak output at 2,100 rpm and above.

Preliminary Generator Test

1. Start the engine and bring the speed up to about 2,500 rpm.

2. Switch on the lights and disconnect battery ground lead. The brightness of the headlight should increase slightly.

3. Reconnect the ground lead. The light should decrease in brightness slightly. If the light performs the opposite in either case, the generator ouuput current is insufficient and the generator should be thoroughly checked.

No-Load Regulating Voltage Test

1. Start the engine and bring the speed up to about 2,000 rpm.

2. Disconnect the battery ground lead and connect a voltmeter between terminal D+61, on the voltage regulator, and ground.

CAUTION
Make sure the voltmeter leads are secure. Loose connections could result in burned out field coils.

3. Increase the engine speed slowly until the voltage remains constant. This should occur between 7.2 and 7.9 volts (6-volt units), or 13.5 and 14 volts (12-volt units). This is the no-load regulating voltage.

4. If the voltmeter needle vibrates or jumps, indicating incorrect operation, there are several possible causes: generator brushes are too short, they are dirty, or they are sticking in their holders; spring tension on the brushes is not enough to hold them against the commutator; the commutator is out-of-round; there is a break or a short in the armature windings; or the voltage regulator is malfunctioning.

Other test parameters, such as cut-in voltage, generator load regulating voltage, and reverse current, should be left to an authorized Bosch service specialist. Precision testers and special equipment are required to perform these tests and correct out-of-specification conditions.

If the preliminary or no-load tests indicate a malfunction, proceed with the following. If the problem is still present, the charging system should be professionally checked.

Generator Disassembly

Removal of the generator from the engine is covered in Chapter Four, *Engine Removal*. Every 6,000 miles, dust from the carbon brushes should be wiped off the commutator and armature with a clean cloth moistened with gasoline.

Generator Inspection

1. Check the condition of the brushes. They should slide easily in their holders and the hold-down springs·should exert about one pound of pressure on the brushes.

2. Check the commutator. If it is scored or worn, it should be turned down on a lathe. This is a job for an expert.

3. Check the runout of the commutator with the armature installed on the shaft. If it is more than 0.04mm (0.0016 in.), it must be turned on a lathe.

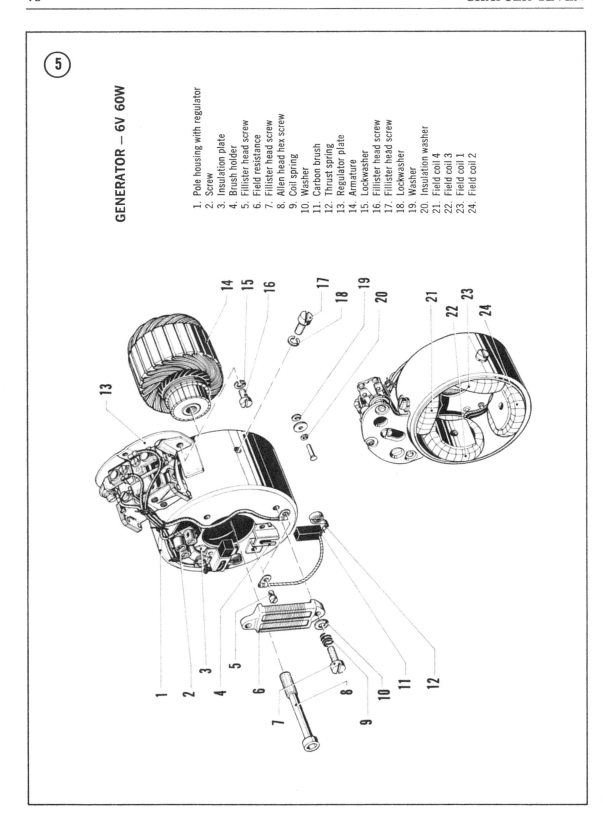

(5)

GENERATOR — 6V 60W

1. Pole housing with regulator
2. Screw
3. Insulation plate
4. Brush holder
5. Fillister head screw
6. Field resistance
7. Fillister head screw
8. Allen head hex screw
9. Coil spring
10. Washer
11. Carbon brush
12. Thrust spring
13. Regulator plate
14. Armature
15. Lockwasher
16. Fillister head screw
17. Fillister head screw
18. Lockwasher
19. Washer
20. Insulation washer
21. Field coil 4
22. Field coil 3
23. Field coil 1
24. Field coil 2

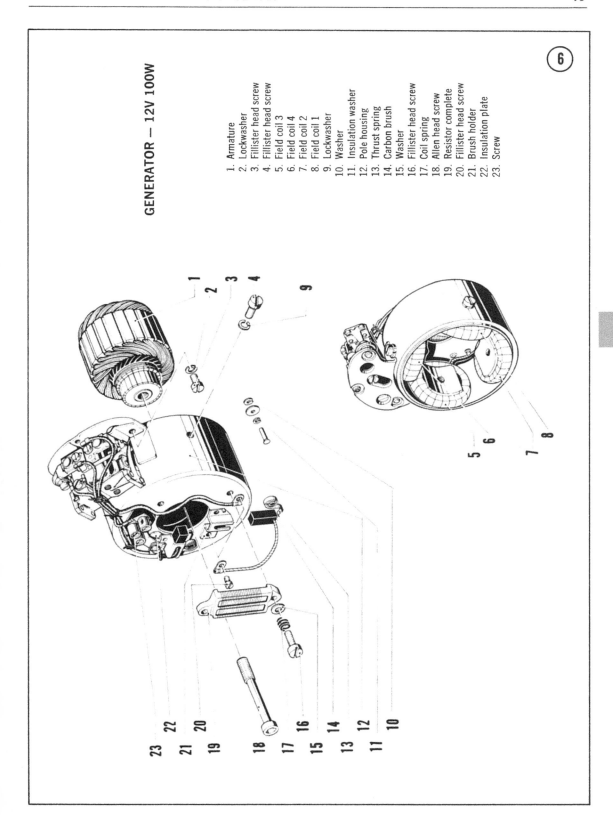

GENERATOR — 12V 100W

1. Armature
2. Lockwasher
3. Fillister head screw
4. Fillister head screw
5. Field coil 3
6. Field coil 4
7. Field coil 2
8. Field coil 1
9. Lockwasher
10. Washer
11. Insulation washer
12. Pole housing
13. Thrust spring
14. Carbon brush
15. Washer
16. Fillister head screw
17. Coil spring
18. Allen head screw
19. Resistor complete
20. Fillister head screw
21. Brush holder
22. Insulation plate
23. Screw

NOTE: *If the commutator is turned down, the brushes should be replaced with new ones.*

4. Inspect the commutator contact segments for badly burned spots. This generally indicates an open circuit in the windings.

5. Check to see if the armature is grounded. Place one probe of a continuity light on a commutator segment, and the other on a segment of the armature. If the light does not light, the armature's insulation against ground is all right. If the light does light, the armature should be replaced.

6. Have the armature professionally checked for shorts in the windings. Replace it if any are found. At the same time, have the field coils checked for resistance, grounding, shorts, and open circuits. If it is found defective, replace it.

Reassembly

Reassemble and reinstall the generator in accordance with instructions in Chapter Four.

Voltage Regulator

The voltage regulator, shown in **Figures 7 and 8**, is a single-field, double-contact type with 2 armatures—one for the voltage regulator, and one for the cutout relay. The regulator is not adjustable, and if it is found faulty it should be replaced, or inspected and serviced by an authorized Bosch service center.

CHARGING SYSTEM (OPTIONAL ALTERNATOR)

This charging system consists of a 3-phase alternator, a diode-type rectifier, and a mechanical voltage regulator (**Figure 9**). The alternator is driven off the end of the crankshaft.

The rotor is an electromagnet, rather than a permanent magnet, and is energized by a demand signal from the regulator through contact brushes and slip rings.

Testing Charging Circuit

1. Check the battery and make sure it is charged to its normal range.

2. Start the engine and bring its speed up to about 1,000 rpm.

3. Disconnect the battery ground lead and connect a voltmeter between the indicator light terminal D+ (blue lead) on the regulator and ground.

4. Increase the engine speed to about 2,000 rpm, and check the reading on the voltmeter. It should be between 13.5 and 14.2 volts.

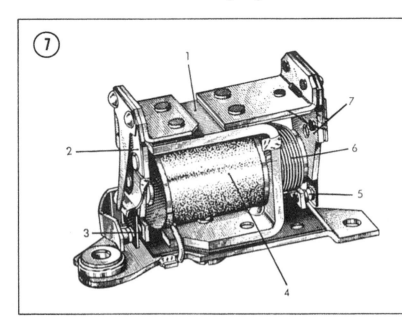

⑦

VOLTAGE REGULATOR

1. Magnet "U" bow
2. Regulator armature
3. Regulator contact points
4. Voltage regulator coil
5. Circuit breaker points
6. Current regulator coil
7. Circuit breaker armature

⑧

VOLTAGE REGULATOR

1. Magnet "U" bow
2. Regulator armature
3. Regulator contact points
4. Voltage regulator coil
5. Circuit breaker points
6. Current regulator coil
7. Circuit breaker armature
8. Magnet core
9. Regulator resistance
10. Generator
11. Charge indicator lamp
12. Ignition switch
13. Battery

⑨

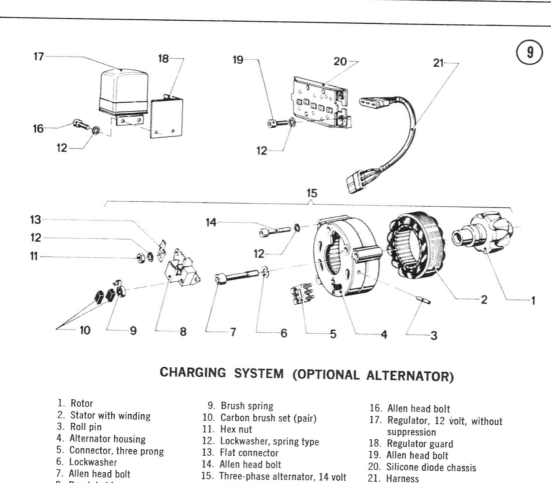

CHARGING SYSTEM (OPTIONAL ALTERNATOR)

1. Rotor
2. Stator with winding
3. Roll pin
4. Alternator housing
5. Connector, three prong
6. Lockwasher
7. Allen head bolt
8. Brush holder
9. Brush spring
10. Carbon brush set (pair)
11. Hex nut
12. Lockwasher, spring type
13. Flat connector
14. Allen head bolt
15. Three-phase alternator, 14 volt
16. Allen head bolt
17. Regulator, 12 volt, without suppression
18. Regulator guard
19. Allen head bolt
20. Silicone diode chassis
21. Harness

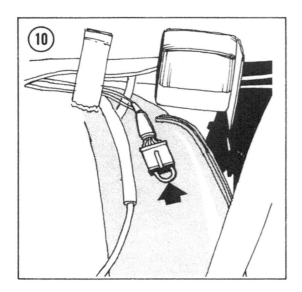

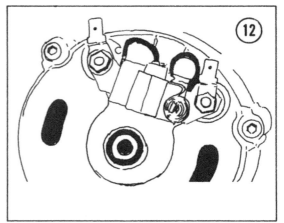

5. Turn on the main light switch and turn the headlight to high beam. Again, check the voltmeter. It should read between 13.9 and 14.8.

Alternator Preliminary Test

If the charge indicator light remains lit when the engine is running and the battery is known to be in good condition, a simple test can be made to determine if the trouble is in the regulator or the alternator.

1. Unplug the electrical connector from the voltage regulator and bridge the D+ (blue) contact and the DF (black) contact with a short piece of insulated wire (**Figure 10**).

2. Start the engine and run it at 1,000-2,000 rpm. If the charge indicator light goes off, the trouble is in the regulator. If the light remains on, the trouble is in the alternator.

Alternator Disassembly

1. Remove the front engine cover (**Figure 11**).

2. Pull the 3-prong plug from the stator. Lift the exciter brushes part way out of their holders and jam them in place with their springs (**Figure 12**).

3. Unscrew the Allen bolts from the stator housing and remove it (**Figure 13**).

4. Unscrew the bolt from the center of the armature and press it off the shaft with a puller (BMW tool No. 5030). See **Figure 14**.

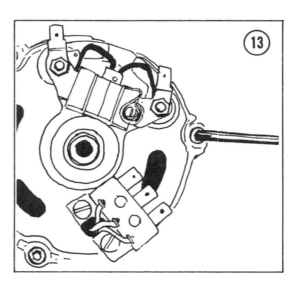

5. Remove the two 8mm hex nuts from the inside of the stator housing and remove the brush holder and brushes.

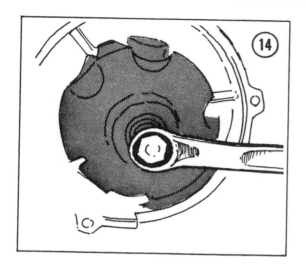

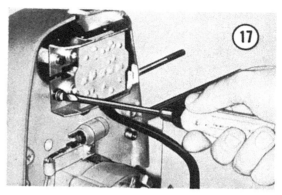

diameter of the slip rings is 26.8mm (1.055 in.). Maximum permissible out-of-round of the slip ring is 0.06mm (0.0024 in.). See **Figure 15**.

2. Check the conditions of the brushes. They should slide easily in their holders, and the hold-down springs should hold them firmly against the slip rings.

Alternator Reassembly

1. If the brushes are replaced, make sure that solder does not run down into the wires.

2. Place the insulator bushing on the stud on the brush holder (**Figure 16**), install the insulator washers, and then reassemble the brush holder and the stator housing.

3. Reassemble the rotor and stator in reverse order of disassembly.

Rectifier Disassembly

Silicon diodes are used to rectify the AC produced by the alternator to DC for storage in the battery and operation of the components of the electrical system. A rectifier is a biased electrical device. It permits current to flow in only one direction. The rectifier performs its function by allowing the alternating current to flow in only one direction, cancelling the reverse pulse and thus rectifying the current to DC.

Because of the rectifier's bias, care must be taken during testing to hook up the test leads and the test battery in correct polarity. Failure to do this will result in a damaged rectifier.

1. Unscrew the 4 mounting screws and remove the diode rectifier chassis (**Figure 17**).

2. Withdraw the plug from the rectifier.

Alternator Inspection

1. Check the armature slip rings for scoring. If necessary, have them turned in a lathe to a high finish. This is a job for an expert. Maximum

Rectifier Testing

Use a service tester to check the continuity of the rectifier. Do not use a megger because the diodes may be damaged by the instrument's high voltage.

1. Test the rectifier for continuity in both directions.

2. Continuity in one direction indicates the rectifier is in good condition. Continuity in both directions, or in neither direction, indicates the rectifier is defective.

Rectifier Reassembly

1. Insert the plug into the rectifier chassis.

2. Hold the rectifier in place on the timing case and reinstall the 4 screws.

Voltage Regulator

The voltage regulator (**Figure 18**) is not adjustable. If a test of the charging circuit indicates the regulator may be defective, it should be removed and replaced or inspected and serviced by an authorized Bosch service center.

BATTERY

The battery in most models is rated at 6 volts, with a capacity of 8 ampere-hours. The battery for other models is rated at 12 volts, with a capacity of 15 ampere-hours. The electrolyte level should be checked regularly, as described in Chapter Three.

Removal

1. Remove the seat.

2. Remove the rubber hold-down strap and remove the leads from the battery terminals—first the negative (ground), and then the positive. See **Figure 19**.

3. Lift the battery out of its holder. Be careful not to spill the corrosive electrolyte.

Inspection

1. Clean the terminals and clamps with a solution of baking soda and water.

2. Check the level of the electrolyte. It should be about 6mm (¼ in.) above the top of the

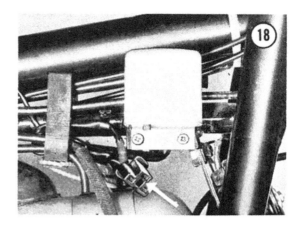

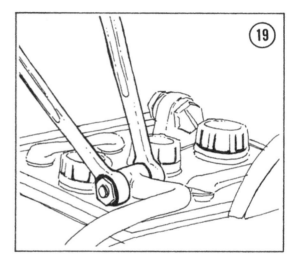

plates. Top up any cells that are low, using only distilled water.

3. Measure the specific gravity of the electrolyte with a hydrometer, reading it as shown in **Figure 20**. Generally, the specific gravity should be between 1.26 and 1.28. If it is less than 1.189 at 68°F (20°C), the battery should be charged. Specific gravity varies with ambient temperature.

Battery Charging

A trickle charger is recommended for restoring a low-voltage battery. Most inexpensive automotive type chargers have a charging rate between 2 and 6 amperes.

A "quick charge" should never be applied to a fully discharged battery, and only seldom to one that is partially discharged; the heat resulting from a quick charge is harmful to the battery.

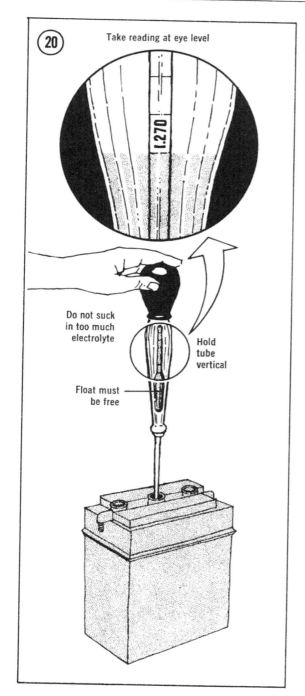

⑳ Take reading at eye level

1.270

Do not suck in too much electrolyte

Hold tube vertical

Float must be free

1. Connect the positive charger lead to the positive battery terminal, and the negative lead to the negative terminal. Reversing the leads can result in damage to both the charger and the battery.

2. Remove the vent caps from the battery, select 6 or 12 volts on the charger, and switch it on. The battery should remain on the charger for about 10 hours, and not less than 8 if it is to receive a full charge. If the output of the charger is adjustable, it is best to select a low setting— about 1½-2 amps.

3. After a suitable charging period (8-10 hours), switch off the charger, disconnect the battery, and check the specific gravity. It should be within 1.26-1.28. If it is, and if after an hour's time the reading is the same, the battery is charged.

Installation

1. Make sure the battery terminals, cable clamps, and case are free of corrosion. Check the rubber pad in the battery case and replace it if it is excessively compressed or rotted.

2. Install the battery in reverse order of removal. Be careful to route the vent tube so that it is not crimped. Connect the positive terminal first, then the negative terminal. Do not overtighten the clamp bolts, but make them snug enough so the clamps cannot be rotated on the terminals.

3. Coat the terminals with a silicon spray, or Vaseline, to retard decomposition of the lead.

7

CHAPTER EIGHT

FRONT SUSPENSION AND STEERING

Two distinctly different front suspension designs are used in BMW twins—the Earles type leading link, and the more common telescopic fork. Because of their differences, they are covered separately in this chapter.

EARLES TYPE LEADING LINK FRONT SUSPENSION

The leading link front suspension is shown in **Figure 1A, 1B, and 1C**. Refer to these exploded views when disassembling and reassembling the suspension unit.

Spring Shocks Disassembly

1. Set the motorcycle on its centerstand and place a block beneath the front of the engine.

2. Remove the nuts and bolts at the top and bottom of each spring/shock unit (**Figure 2**) and remove the unit.

3. Place the ring of the compression tool (BMW tool No. 5094) over the upper spring tube of the shock and clamp the upper mounting lug of the shock in a vise. Insert the pin of the fixture in the mounting hole in the bottom of the shock and pull the fixture handle over center to compress the spring (**Figure 3**). Place a 9mm open-end wrench on the exposed flats of the damper rod and unscrew it.

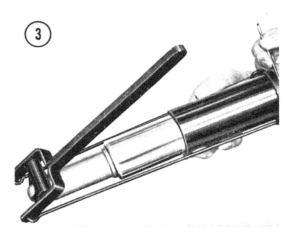

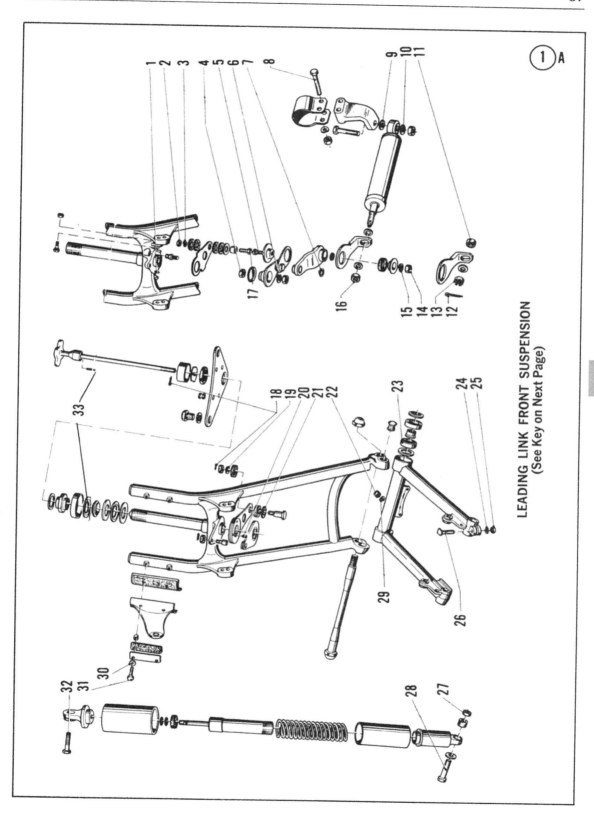

LEADING LINK FRONT SUSPENSION
(See Key on Next Page)

1 A

LEADING LINK FRONT SUSPENSION
(See Previous Page)

1. Tension sleeve
2. Hex nut
3. Spring washer
4. Hex nut
5. Fillister head screw
6. Lockwasher
7. Snap ring
8. Hex head screw
9. Washer
10. Spring washer
11. Hex nut
12. Split pin
13. Castle nut
14. Hex nut
15. Lockwasher
16. Hex nut
17. Hex head screw
18. Split pin
19. Washer
20. Rivet
21. Washer
22. Lubrication nipple
23. Ball bearing
24. Shakeproof washer
25. Hex nut
26. Clamping screw
27. Hex nut
28. Hex head screw
29. Seal ring
30. Shakeproof washer
31. Hex head screw
32. Hex head screw
33. Ball

1 B

LEADING LINK FRONT SUSPENSION

1. Lock cap
2. Hex head screw
3. Thrust spring
4. Thumb screw
5. Bearing bolt
6. Rubber washer
7. Spacer tube
8. Resistance plate
9. Control joint
10. Arresting lever
11. Clamp
12. Support
13. N. A.
14. Retaining plate
15. Attachment bracket
16. Steering damper
17. Guide ring
18. Spacer washer
19. Safety washer
20. Lower nut
21. Lock cap
22. Rubber ring
23. Resistance plate
24. Retaining screw
25. Silent bloc
26. Telescopic leg eye, lower
27. Cover, lower
28. Suspension spring
29. Shock absorber
30. Stop ring
31. Cover, upper
32. Telescopic eye, upper

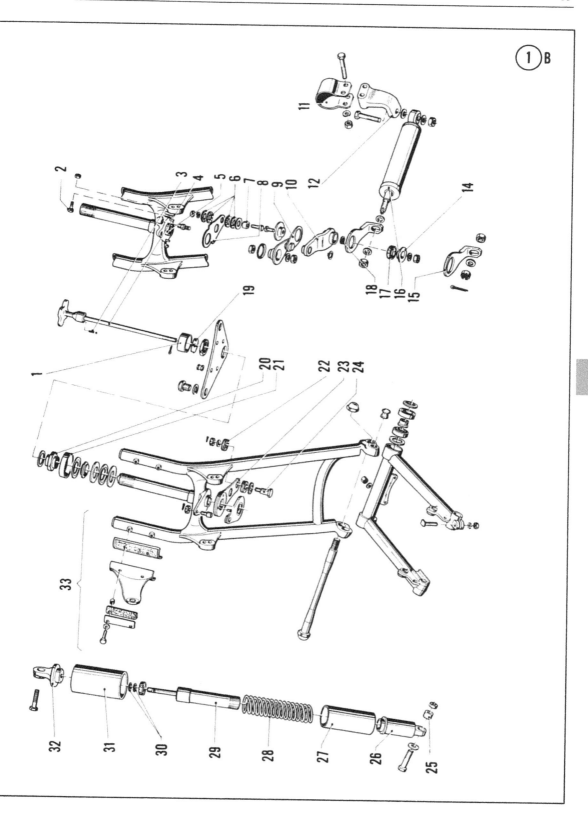

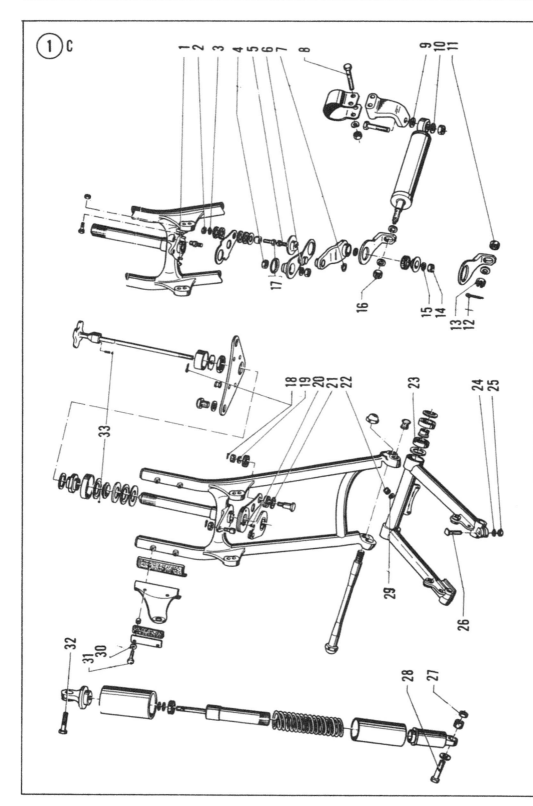

LEADING LINK FRONT SUSPENSION

1. Tension sleeve
2. Hex nut
3. Spring washer
4. Hex nut
5. Fillister head screw
6. Lockwasher
7. Snap ring
8. Hex head screw
9. Washer
10. Spring washer
11. Hex nut
12. Split pin
13. Castle nut
14. Hex nut
15. Lockwasher
16. Hex nut
17. Hex head screw
18. Split pin
19. Washer
20. Rivet
21. Washer
22. Lubrication nipple
23. Ball bearing
24. Shakeproof washer
25. Hex nut
26. Clamping screw
27. Hex nut
28. Hex head screw
29. Seal ring
30. Shakeproof washer
31. Hex head screw
32. Hex head screw
33. Ball

4. Clamp the eye of the lower shock leg into a vise. Remove the upper protecting cap and unscrew the shock absorber top with a clamping wrench (Dowidat tool No. 31.10). See **Figure 4**.

5. Pull damper assembly out of shock leg.

Inspection

1. Measure the free length of the spring with a vernier caliper. If the length of the spring is significantly less than 284mm (11.18 in.), replace it.

2. Hold the shock absorber upright, in its operating position, and pump it in and out several times to displace the air to the upper chamber.

3. Test the relationship of compression and rebound damping by first compressing the shock absorber, then extending it. Noticeably less compression force should be required than extension force. Also, the shaft should move smoothly and steadily, requiring the same force throughout the length of the stroke. If the stroke is uneven, the shock is worn and should be replaced.

If the force required to compress the shock is about the same as that required to extend it, the shock is worn and requires replacement. The test stroke is 25mm (0.9854 in.). The compression force should be 11 pounds, and the extension force should be 33 pounds.

CAUTION
With the shock fully compressed, no more than one pound of pressure should be exerted on the shaft; more than this can cause internal damage.

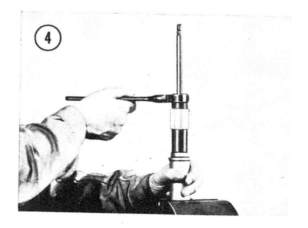

Reassembly

Reassemble the spring/shock in the reverse order of disassembly.

Swinging Arm Disassembly

1. With the motorcycle on its centerstand and blocked up, and with the spring/shocks removed, disconnect the front brake cable from the backing plate.

2. Loosen the axle pinch bolts on either side of the swinging arm, unscrew the axle nut, pull out the axle, and remove the wheel.

3. Remove the front fender.

4. Unscrew the acorn nut on the left side of the swinging arm pivot and screw the pilot pin (BMW tool No. 519) into the end of the pivot bolt. Tap and pull the bolt completely out (**Figure 5**).

5. Remove the swinging arm and the right and left shims.

6. Remove the bearing seal, thrust bushing and inner race, and the roller cage, from both sides.

7. Check the condition of the outer bearing races which are pressed into the swinging arm. If they are in good condition, leave them in place. If they are pitted, galled, or worn, remove them. Use a common internal bearing race puller, or tap them out from the opposite side with a long drift. If they are tapped out with a drift, both the inner washers and the races will have to be replaced.

NOTE: *Do not mix the right and left races, rollers, or bushings.*

Inspection

1. Check the bearings and races for wear or damage and replace them if necessary.

2. Check the bearing seals for damage and replace them if necessary.

Reassembly

1. Pack the swinging arm pivot tube and the roller bearings with a good grade of bearing grease.

2. Screw the pilot pin into the end of the pivot bolt. Screw the knurled pilot pin nut into the thread on the left pivot of the fork.

3. Reinstall the races, bearings, bushings, and seals in the ends of the swinging arm pivot.

4. Put the swinging arm in place, between the lower fork legs, and reinsert the shims.

NOTE: *Side play of the swinging arm in the fork should be no more than 0.1mm (0.0039 in.). If necessary, use thicker shims.*

5. Insert the pivot bolt into the fork and swinging arm (**Figure 6**) and tap it in carefully until it contacts the end of the knurled nut. Partially unscrew the knurled nut and screw in the pivot bolt until its threads have caught the threads in the left fork leg. Then, unscrew the knurled nut completely and screw in the pivot bolt all the way (**Figure 7**).

6. Tighten the pivot bolt and the acorn nut, so that with the front wheel removed the swinging arm will fall slowly, to about 50 degrees, under its own weight.

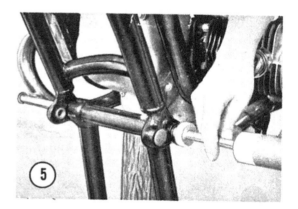

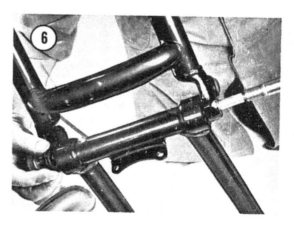

7. Reinstall the fender, wheel, brake cable, and spring/shocks in reverse order of their disassembly.

Front Fork Disassembly

Remove the wheel, spring/shocks, fender, and swinging arm as outlined previously.

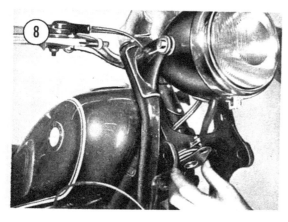

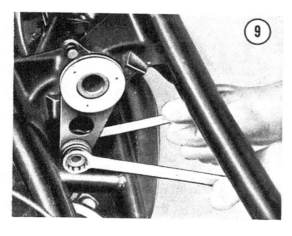

On models equipped with a friction type steering damper, refer to **Figure 1** and proceed as follows.

1. Remove the cotter pin from the bottom end of the damper rod.

2. Unscrew the rod with the damper knob (**Figure 8**) and remove the bottom pressure plate and top lock cap and washer.

3. Remove the cotter pin from the castellated nut and bolt holding the bottom pressure plate in place, unscrew the nut, and remove the plate.

4. Do the same with the friction plate and remove it along with its spring washer, flat washers, and rubber rings (**Figure 9**).

On models equipped with a hydraulic steering damper, refer to **Figures 10A and 10B** and proceed as follows.

1. With a thin-wall, 12mm socket unscrew the bottom nut (**Figure 11**). Pull the lock knob out of the steering head.

2. Remove the nut from the end of the steering damper shaft (**Figure 12**). To prevent the shaft from rotating, hold it with a screwdriver inserted in the end slot.

3. Remove the arresting lever and control joint.

4. Unscrew the bolt holding the damper to the rear bracket and remove the bracket. Unless absolutely necessary, do not remove or loosen the support arm which connects to the top frame tube. The position of this piece is critical to the correct adjustment of the steering damper. If the support is disturbed, it must be relocated as outlined later.

5. Disconnect the headlight dimmer switch (left) and the directional signal switch (right) from the handlebars (**Figure 13**).

6. Pull the wiring harness part way out of the headlight shell. Unscrew the mounting bolts and carefully remove the rubber washers. To protect the headlight from damage, wrap it in several thicknesses of newspaper and slip a paper bag over it. Tape the neck of the bag closed around the wiring harness.

7. Unscrew the 36mm nut in the center of the upper fork guide, and the 19mm nuts on either side of it.

8. Cover the fuel tank with a clean cloth, lift off

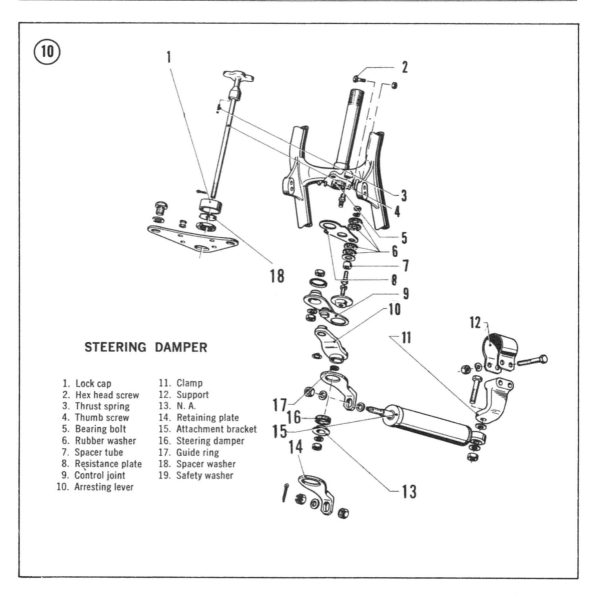

STEERING DAMPER

1. Lock cap
2. Hex head screw
3. Thrust spring
4. Thumb screw
5. Bearing bolt
6. Rubber washer
7. Spacer tube
8. Resistance plate
9. Control joint
10. Arresting lever
11. Clamp
12. Support
13. N. A.
14. Retaining plate
15. Attachment bracket
16. Steering damper
17. Guide ring
18. Spacer washer
19. Safety washer

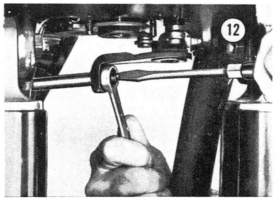

the plate with the handlebars attached, and place them on the tank.

9. Remove the shim from the 41mm steering head nut and unscrew it (**Figure 14**). Be careful not to lose any ball bearings as the fork drops down and out of the steering head.

10. Remove the top protection cap, the outer race, and the balls.

> NOTE: *Do not mix the balls from the bottom race with the balls from the top race.*

Inspection

1. On friction dampers, check the thrust spring, damper washer, and the rubber rings for wear. Replace them if necessary.

2. With the hydraulic damper in the installed position—horizontal, with the notch at the rear facing down (**Figure 15**)—move the rod in and out to check for even resistance. Resistance should be the same in both directions. If the resistance varies from one direction to the other, the damper should be replaced. See **Table 1**.

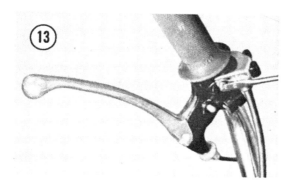

> NOTE: *If the damper is tested in a shock absorber tester, it must meet the standards given in **Table 1**.*

3. Check the bearings and races for wear, pitting, and galling. Replace them if necessary.

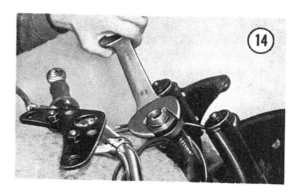

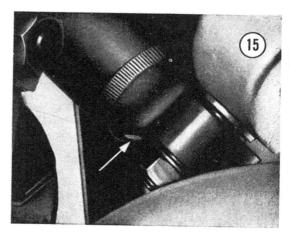

Notch (arrow)

Table 1   FRONT SHOCK ABSORBER STANDARDS

Damper Diameter	31mm (1.220 in.)		24mm (0.945 in.)	
Length of Test Stroke	25mm (0.98 in.)	50mm (1.97 in.)	25mm (0.98 in.)	50mm (1.97 in.)
Test rate, strokes per minute	100	100	100	100
Tensile force (extension), lb.	66	73	50	77
Pressure force (compression), lb.	66	73	50	77
Maximum length, center of bushing to rod end	230mm (9.055 in.)	230mm (9.055 in.)	250mm (9.843 in.)	250mm (9.843 in.)
Minimum length	171mm (6.732 in.)	171mm (6.732 in.)	192mm (7.59 in.)	192mm (7.59 in.)

Reassembly

1. Grease the balls and replace them in their respective races. There should be 23 balls in each race. Liberally grease the inner bearing races in the steering head.

2. Insert the fork pivot into the steering head and guide it carefully into place. Replace the top bearing race and the protective cap, and screw on the top nut. Tighten the nut until all end play is removed, but the fork still turns freely.

3. Reinstall the upper fork guide, the headlight, and the switches.

4. Refer to **Figure 1** and reinstall the friction damper in reverse order of disassembly. The pieces are pre-located and require no adjustment, other than that of the thumb screw for individual preference of damping resistance.

Hydraulic Steering Damper

NOTE: *The hydraulic steering damper has several preliminary adjustments which must be made during installation. If the damper is not correctly installed and precisely adjusted, the motorcycle's handling can be adversely affected to the point that safety is compromised. Follow the next steps closely, and double check all your work against the instructions.*

1. Reassemble the steering damper in reverse order of disassembly. The 14mm nut on the thumb screw shaft above the control joint must be adjusted so that when the 12mm bottom nut is tightened all the way, the spring washer is compressed and will still allow the thumb screw to be rotated. Check to see that the end of the thumb screw shaft does not protrude downward far enough to contact with arresting lever.

NOTE: *The notch at the rear of the damper cylinder must face down (**Figure 15**). Do not install the damper rod in the control joint.*

2. Turn the thumb screw to the disengaged position. Adjust the limiting bolt (**Figure 16**) so that the arresting lever makes contact with it just after the detent point is felt. When the thumb screw is disengaged (the red dot must point to the rear), it is held in position by 2 spring-loaded detent balls which drop into depressions in the lock cap. The tension sleeve limits the movement of the control joint.

3. With the rear cylinder support loose on the top frame tube, engage the damper thumb screw.

4. Carefully pull the damper rod out until it stops in the cylinder. Measure the distance from the cylinder to the beginning of the threads on the rod. It should be about 62mm (2.44 in.).

5. Carefully push the rod all the way into the cylinder and then draw it out 6 to 9mm (0.236 to 0.354 in.). See **Figure 17**.

6. Slip a flat washer over the end of the rod.

7. Turn the fork all the way to the left and guide the oblong hole in the control lever over the end

A. Limit screw   a. Tension sleeve

b. 6-9mm (0.236-0.355 in.)

of the rod. Install the outer washer and the nut. If the rod was fitted with a self-locking nut, replace it with a new one.

8. While maintaining the 6-9mm distance between the cylinder and the washer on the rod, tighten the cylinder support on the frame tube. It may be necessary to move the end of the rod up in the oblong hole to prevent the cylinder from contacting the fork leg (**Figure 18**).

9. With the damper disengaged, turn the fork all the way to the right and measure the length of rod (**Figure 19**). It should be 57mm (2.24 in.), and must be less than its total extended length in Step 4 above. If it is not, loosen the cylinder support and carefully move it forward or back until the length is correct.

10. Move the thumb screw to the engaged position and check to see that the cylinder does not contact the fork leg.

11. Recheck the measurements and clearances.

NOTE: *The procedure may have to be repeated several times until the damper is correctly adjusted. Be patient and thorough; accuracy is essential to good handling and safety.*

12. Reassemble the rest of the front end in reverse order of disassembly. Adjust the headlight beam in accordance with the instructions in Chapter Thirteen.

TELESCOPIC FRONT SUSPENSION

The telescopic front suspension for late models is shown in **Figures 20 and 21**. Refer to

these exploded views when disassembling and reassembling the front end.

Damping Oil

The damping oil in the front fork should be changed every 8,000 miles or once a year, or at anytime excessive bouncing of the front end indicates a low oil level. Changing of the damping oil is described in Chapter Three.

Steering Damper—Friction Type Disassembly

1. Remove the circlip from the bottom of the damper rod and unscrew the damper knob (**Figure 22**).

2. Remove knob, spring washer, pressure plate, and rubber guide ring inside the center tube.

3. Unscrew the Allen bolt from the frame (**Figure 23**) and remove the damper plate.

Steering Damper—Friction Type Inspection and Reassembly

Check the contact surfaces of the friction damper and replace the unit if they are excessively worn, pitted, or galled. Reassemble the damper in reverse order of disassembly.

Front Fork Removal

1. Place the motorcycle on the centerstand and block up the front until the front wheel is off the ground (**Figure 24**).

2. On models equipped with a drum brake, disconnect the brake cable from the brake arm and the backing plate. Remove the cotter key

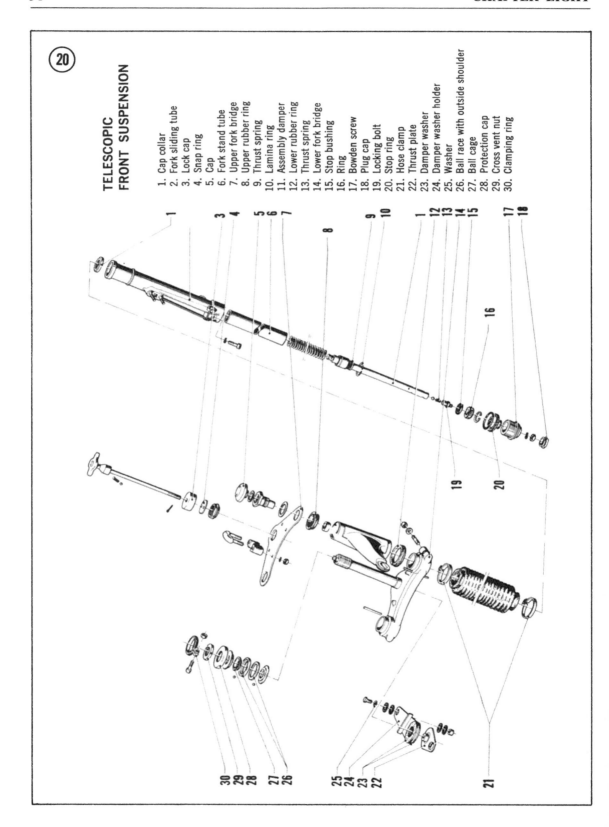

**TELESCOPIC
FRONT SUSPENSION**

1. Cap collar
2. Fork sliding tube
3. Lock cap
4. Snap ring
5. Cap
6. Fork stand tube
7. Upper fork bridge
8. Upper rubber ring
9. Thrust spring
10. Lamina ring
11. Assembly damper
12. Lower rubber ring
13. Thrust spring
14. Lower fork bridge
15. Stop bushing
16. Ring
17. Bowden screw
18. Plug cap
19. Locking bolt
20. Stop ring
21. Hose clamp
22. Thrust plate
23. Damper washer
24. Damper washer holder
25. Washer
26. Ball race with outside shoulder
27. Ball cage
28. Protection cap
29. Cross vent nut
30. Clamping ring

TELESCOPIC FRONT SUSPENSION

1. Stud
2. Spring washer
3. Fillister head screw
4. Fork suspension spring
5. Upper rubber ring
6. Headlight bracket
7. Headlight bracket
8. Ball
9. Circlip
10. Seal ring
11. Seal ring
12. Spring washer
13. Hex nut
14. Washer
15. Stud
16. Mera hose clamp
17. Rubber boot
18. Spacer tube
19. Rubber washer
20. Hex head screw
21. Tension sleeve
22. Washer
23. Ball race with inside shoulder
24. Ball
25. Hex nut
26. Fillister head screw
27. Spring
28. Ball
29. Cotter pin
30. Thumb screw (damper knob)
31. Centering nut
32. Upper clamping support
33. Lower clamping support
34. Upper spring bearing
35. Seal ring
36. Shim
37. Spring washer
38. Hex nut

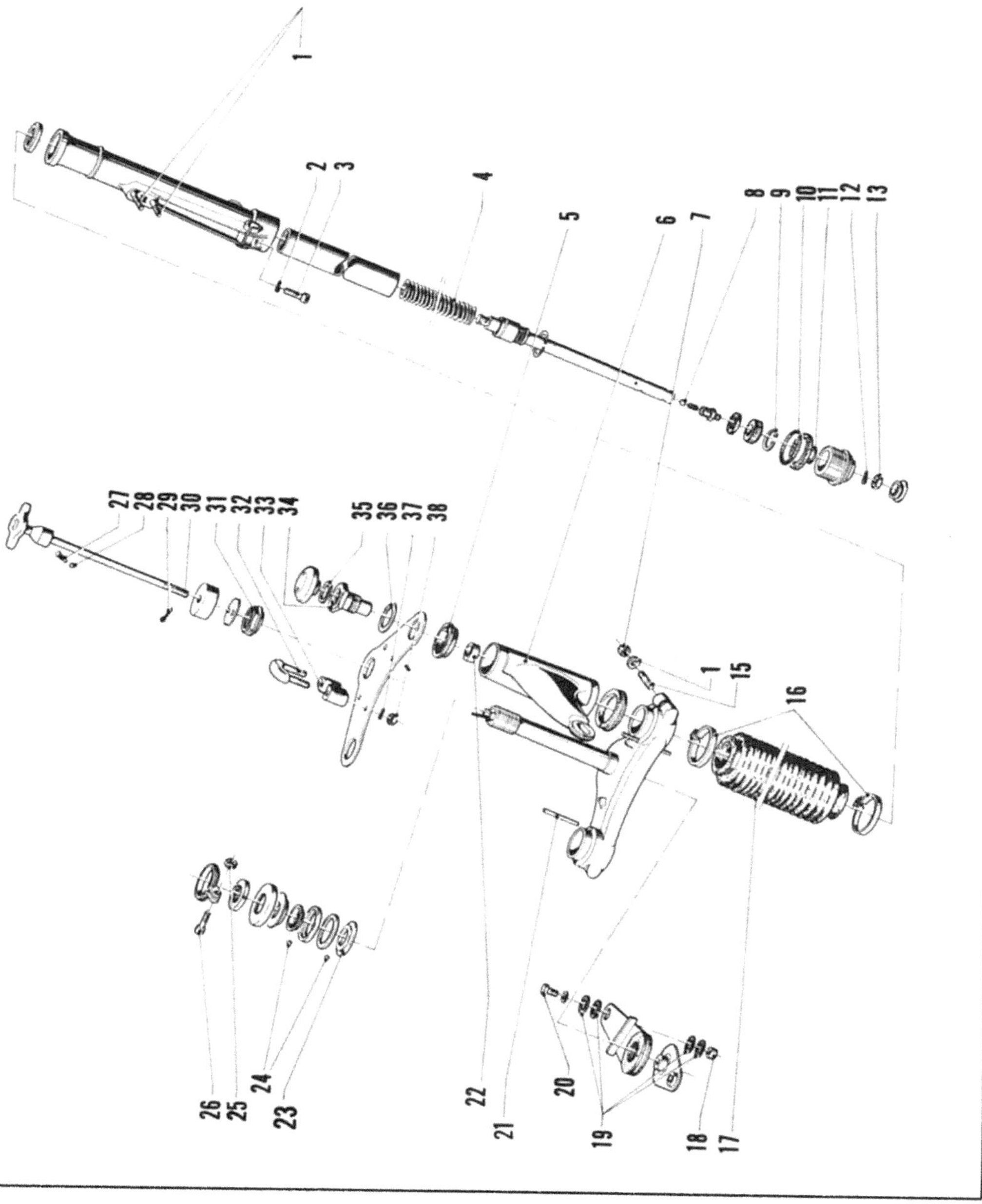

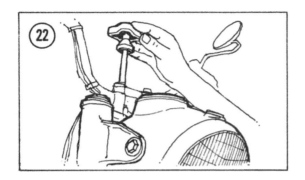

1. Axle nut   2. Pinch bolt   3. Axl

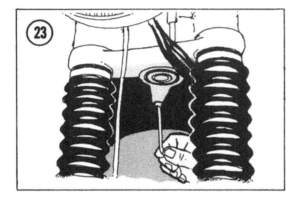

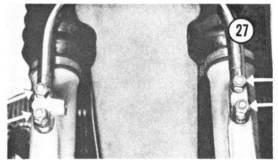

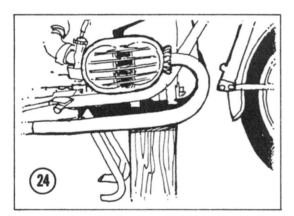

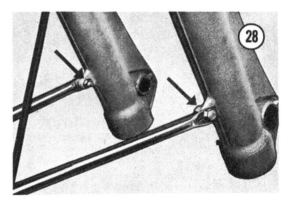

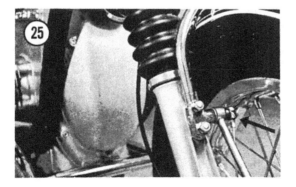

and nut from the brake anchor bolt and remove the bolt (**Figure 25**).

3. Unscrew the axle nut, loosen the pinch bolt, and pull out the axle (**Figure 26**). Remove the front wheel and brake assembly.

4. Unscrew the 4 self-locking nuts from the upper fender brace (**Figure 27**).

5. Unscrew the nuts and bolts from the lower fender braces (**Figure 28**) and remove the front fender.

6. Remove the steering damper.

7. Disconnect the battery ground cable.

8. Remove headlight mounting bolts, washers, and grommets. Wrap the headlight in several thicknesses of newspaper, place a paper bag over it, and tape the neck of the bag closed around the wiring harness.

9. Cover the fuel tank with a clean cloth, remove the handlebar supports from the upper fork bracket (**Figure 29**), and carefully lay the handlebars on the fuel tank.

10. Remove the filler caps from the tops of the fork legs with a pin wrench.

11. Place a small block between the left side fork tops and unscrew the upper spring retainers (**Figure 30**).

12. Unscrew the nut from the top of the steering head (**Figure 31**) and remove the upper fork bracket.

13. Lift off the headlight brackets with their rubber rings (**Figure 32**).

14. Unscrew the crown nut (if fitted). See **Figure 33**. Remove the Allen bolt from the clamp ring and remove the ring (**Figure 34**). Remove the split ring nut and the upper dust cover from the steering head.

15. Pull the fork assembly downward out of the steering head. It may be necessary to tap on the top of the pivot tube with a soft-face mallet.

16. Upend the fork and drain the oil from the legs. Clamp the entire assembly into a vise (**Figure 35**), with a wooden fixture (BMW tool No. 545) or grooved wooden blocks between the vise jaws and the pivot tube.

17. Loosen the 4 clamping bands on the rubber protection boots and slide the boots off the lower fork legs.

18. Remove the rubber caps from the ends of the legs and unscrew the shock absorber retaining nuts while holding the shock absorber bottom bolts with an Allen wrench.

19. Pull off the lower fork legs.

20. Remove the dust covers (**Figure 36**).

21. Remove the gaskets from the bottom of the shock absorber bolts and remove the circlips from the bottom of the fork tubes (**Figure 37**). Then, remove the oil orifices with a pin wrench (**Figure 38**).

22. Pull out the shock absorbers, along with the bottoming rings and the springs (**Figure 39**).

23. Remove the springs from the shock absorbers by twisting them clockwise (**Figure 40**).

24. To remove the fork tubes from the yoke, loosen the yoke pinch bolts, spread the tube bosses with a wedge, and withdraw the tubes.

25. Clamp the hex nut on the bottom of the shock absorber in a vise, and unscrew the spring support and the piston rings. Remove the damper valve and its spring.

26. Clamp the shock absorber tube into a vise, using jaw protectors. Unscrew the retainer and remove the other ball and spring.

Front Fork Inspection

1. If the front fork has been damaged in a collision, carefully examine the bottom fork yoke, top fork clamp, fork tubes, and lower legs for hairline fractures. Replace damaged parts as necessary.

2. Check the fork tubes for runout (**Figure 41**). The maximum allowable runout is 0.1mm

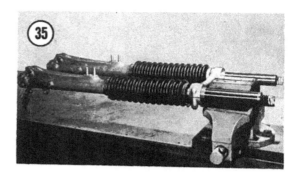

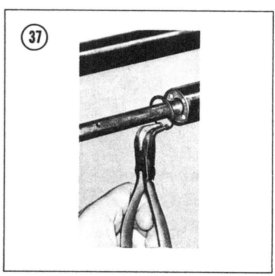

(0.0039 in.). If the runout is more than this, replace the tube.

WARNING
Do not attempt to straighten bent fork tubes. The likelihood of a fracture is very high in a tube which has been bent and straightened.

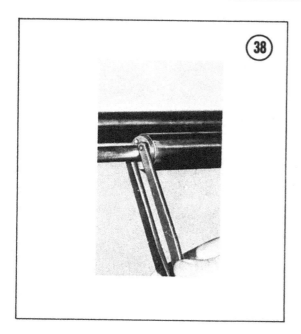

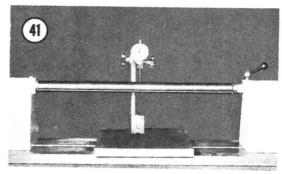

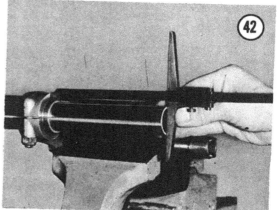

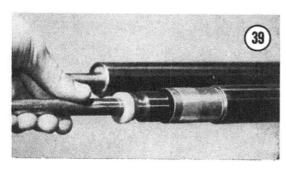

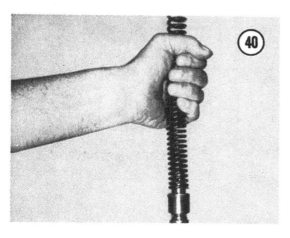

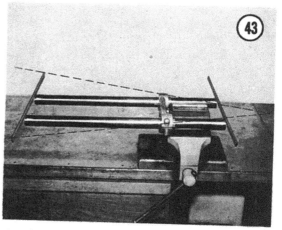

8

3. Install true legs in the lower fork yoke. The distance from the top of the leg to the yoke (**Figure 42**) should be 160mm (6.3 in.).

4. Place 2 straightedges across the ends of the tubes (**Figure 43**) and visually check for distortion or misalignment.

5. With a large caliper, check to see that the tubes are parallel in the yoke.

6. Check the alignment of the steering pivot tube with the fork tubes by installing the upper fork brace, the center nut, and the 2 spring

retainers (**Figure 44**). The nut and retainers must screw on easily, without binding. If any of the above indicates that the lower fork yoke is bent, do not attempt to straighten it. Instead, replace it with a new unit.

7. With an inside micrometer, measure the inside diameter of lower fork leg at its upper end. It should be 28 ± 0.15mm (1.1024 ± 0.0059 in.). With an outside micrometer, measure outside diameter of shock absorber piston. It should be 27.7 ± 0.1mm (1.091 ± 0.0039 in.).

Subtract the piston diameter from the fork leg inside diameter to determine actual clearance. It should be between 0.05 and 0.55mm (0.0020 and 0.0226 in.). If the clearance is excessive, replace the worn component. Most likely, this will be the piston.

8. Check the damper valves for pitting and replace them if necessary. Check the valve springs for tension. If they offer little resistance, they should be replaced.

Front Fork Reassembly

1. Reassemble the shock absorbers in reverse order of disassembly.

2. Clamp the bottom retainer in a vise and tighten both ends of the shock absorber simultaneously (**Figure 45**) by turning the spring retainer nut with a torque wrench. Torque assembly to between 2.5-2.7 mkg (18-19.5 ft.-lb.).

3. Grease the steering head bearings and races. Set the top bearing into its outer race and slide bottom bearing over its inner race (**Figure 46**).

4. Reinstall the lower fork yoke and the top fork clamp in the steering head.

5. Reinstall the dust cover and the split ring nut. Tighten the nut until there is no play. Tap the tube and the yoke to take up any slack as you tighten the nut. Install the clamp ring and tighten the pinch bolt. The fork yoke and clamp assembly should move easily from side to side with no play present along the pivot axis.

6. Slide the fork tubes into the yoke, and reinstall the turn signals and headlight brackets. Push the fork tubes up against the upper bracket (**Figure 47**). Tighten the pinch bolts. Install the

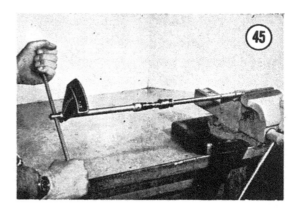

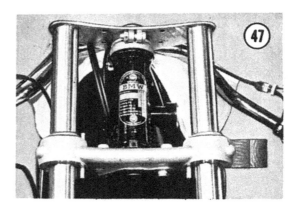

upper spring retainers, and torque them to 12 mkg (87 ft.-lb.).

7. Slide the dust covers onto the fork tubes, making sure the vent pipe in the fork yoke

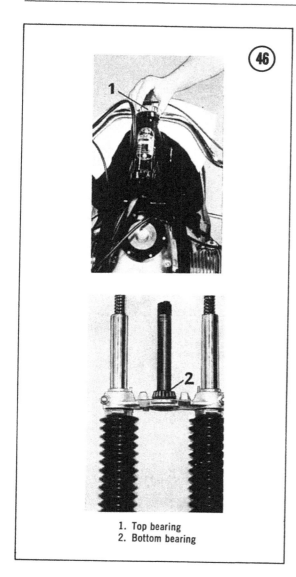

1. Top bearing
2. Bottom bearing

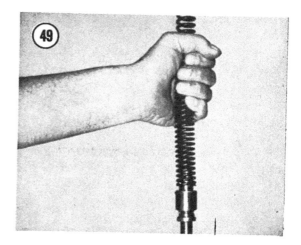

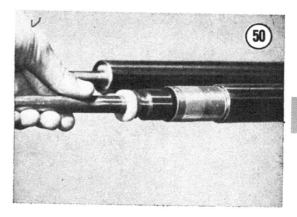

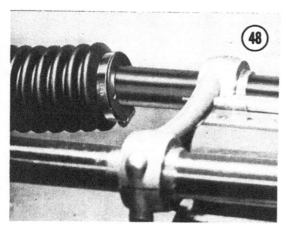

engages the vent hole in the cover (**Figure 48**). Tighten the cover clamping band.

8. Reinstall the springs on the shock absorbers, turning the springs to the right (**Figure 49**).

9. Install new seals in the lower fork legs. Coat the outer edge of each seal with gasket cement and press them in with the mandrel (BMW tool No. 547). See **Figure 50**. The narrow lip and metal edge of the seal must face up.

> NOTE: *If KACO brand seals are used, they must be installed without gasket cement and with the open end facing down.*

10. Slide the springs and shock absorbers into the fork tubes.

11. Compress the shock absorber rings (BMW tool No. 546) and insert the springs and shock

absorbers, with the plastic ring in place, into the fork tubes (**Figure 51**).

12. Reinstall the oil orifice and the circlip.

13. Torque the bottom fork covers to 12-13 mkg (87-94 ft.-lb.).

14. Install new gaskets on the bottom of the shock bolt and reinstall the lower fork legs. Hold the shock absorber bolts with an Allen wrench and tighten the retaining nuts. Torque the nuts to between 2.3-2.6 mkg (16.6-18.8 ft.-lb.).

15. Slide the bottoms of the dust covers onto the legs and tighten the bands.

16. Reinstall the handlebars, switches, headlight, front fender and wheel, and steering damper in reverse order of disassembly. Refer to Chapter Three for filling the forks with oil, to Chapter Thirteen for adjusting headlight, and to Chapter Eleven for adjusting front brake.

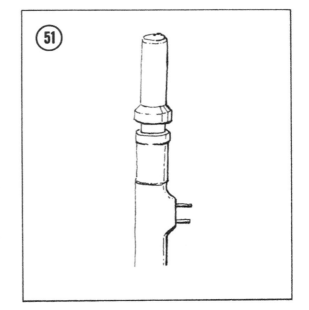

CHAPTER NINE

REAR SUSPENSION

All models have swing arm rear suspensions with hydraulically dampened, coil-spring controlled rear spring/shock absorbers. The spring/shocks connect to the main frame at the base of the upper shock body.

The rear swing arm is covered in Chapter Ten.

The hydraulic damping units on all US models cannot be rebuilt. If they are found faulty, they should be replaced. Spring/shock absorbers are shown in **Figure 1**.

DISASSEMBLY

1. Place the motorcycle on the centerstand.
2. Move tension selector to the SOLO position.
3. Unscrew lower mounting bolts (**Figure 2**).
4. Remove the top cap with a ring spanner. Prevent the shock absorber shaft from turning with a screwdriver and remove the top nut with a ring spanner.
5. Remove the shock absorber and spring downward from the upper mount. The removable components are shown in **Figure 3**.

INSPECTION

1. Measure the free length of the spring with a vernier caliper. If it measures significantly less than 272.5mm (10.728 in.), replace it.

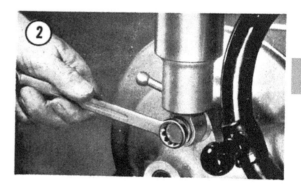

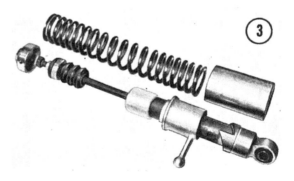

2. Hold the shock absorber in its operating position and pump it in and out several times to displace the air into the upper chamber.
3. Test the relationship of compression and rebound damping by first compressing the shock

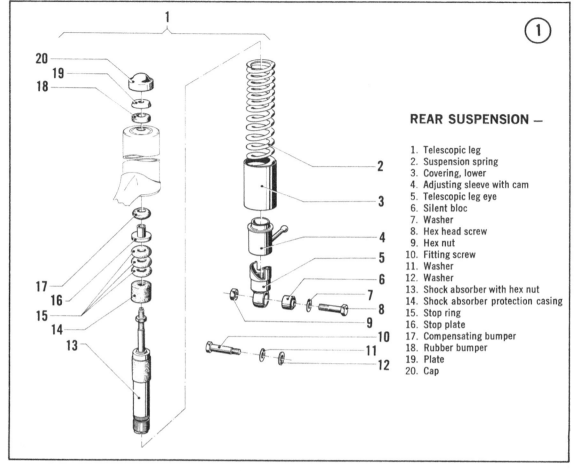

REAR SUSPENSION —

1. Telescopic leg
2. Suspension spring
3. Covering, lower
4. Adjusting sleeve with cam
5. Telescopic leg eye
6. Silent bloc
7. Washer
8. Hex head screw
9. Hex nut
10. Fitting screw
11. Washer
12. Washer
13. Shock absorber with hex nut
14. Shock absorber protection casing
15. Stop ring
16. Stop plate
17. Compensating bumper
18. Rubber bumper
19. Plate
20. Cap

Table 1   SHOCK ABSORBER TEST VALUES

Mode	25mm (0.984 in.) Stroke	75mm (2.953 in.) Stroke
Extension	20 kg (44 lb.)	60 kg (132 lb.)
Compression	5 kg (11 lb.)	20 kg (44 lb.)

absorber and then extending it. The force required for compression should be noticeably less than that for extension. The shaft should move smoothly and steadily, requiring the same force throughout the length of the stroke. If stroke is uneven, the shock should be replaced.

If the force required to compress the shock is about equal to the force required to extend it, or if the extension force is less, the shock is worn and should be replaced. Test values should be comparable to those in **Table 1**.

CAUTION
With the shock fully compressed, no more than one pound of pressure should be exerted on the shaft; more than this can cause internal damage to the unit.

REASSEMBLY

Reassemble and reinstall the spring/shock absorbers in reverse order of disassembly.

CHAPTER TEN

FINAL DRIVE

All BMW models employ a shaft drive to the rear wheel. The drive shaft is housed inside the right rear swing arm and runs in an oil bath. Power is transmitted through a lap-fitted pinion and ring gearset. The final drive is shown in cutaway in **Figure 1**.

DISASSEMBLY

1. Refer to Chapter Eleven and remove the rear wheel.

2. Refer to Chapter Eight and remove the bottom bolt from the right rear spring/shock.

3. Remove the filler and drain plugs from the drive unit (**Figure 2**) and allow the oil to drain.

4. Remove the wing nut from the end of the brake rod and withdraw the rod by depressing the brake pedal.

5. Remove the pin from the brake arm and reinstall it on the rod along with the wing nut (**Figure 3**).

6. Remove the 4 nuts which hold the rear drive to the swing arm (**Figure 4**).

7. Remove the rear drive from the swing arm (**Figure 5**).

8. Refer to **Figure 6** and disconnect the red (right), white (center), and black (left) leads from the terminal block.

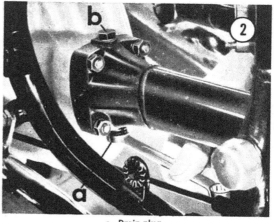

a. Drain plug
b. Fill plug

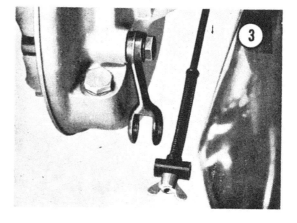

1

FINAL DRIVE

9. Refer to **Figure 7** and remove the 13mm bolt at the bottom front of the rear fender, the two 10mm bolts above the battery holder, and the two 10mm bolts on either side of fender at top of the spring/shock unit. Remove the rear fender.

10. Loosen the screw on the clamping band for the rubber boot at the universal joint (**Figure 8**) and push the boot back as far as it will go.

11. Lock drive shaft with BMW tool No. 508 and unscrew the 4 bolts from the drive shaft coupling (**Figure 9**).

12. Remove the cotter key and castellated nut from the brake bellcrank (**Figure 10**) and remove it from the swing arm.

13. Unscrew the 36mm cap nuts (**Figure 11**) at the front of the swing arm.

14. Loosen the locknut and unscrew the bearing pins with a pin wrench (**Figure 12**).

15. Remove the bottom bolt and nut from the left side spring/shock (**Figure 13**) and remove the swing arm.

16. Refer to **Figure 14**. Remove rubber seals, thrust sleeves, bearings and inner races, and the grease retainers.

17. Clamp the swing arm in a vise, using soft metal jaw protectors. Install the splined fixture (BMW tool No. 508) fitted with a 14mm socket into the internal splines in the rear coupling. Unscrew the nut from the rear of the shaft (**Figure 15**).

18. Install a puller (BMW tool No. 204/2) on the rear coupling (**Figure 16**) and pull it off by turning the puller spindle clockwise. If necessary, rap sharply on the head of the spindle as it is turned.

19. Pull the drive shaft out of the forward end of the swing arm.

20. Mark the brake shoes "top" and "bottom" and remove them by first prying off the shoe that seats beneath the flattened side of the rear collar (**Figure 17**).

21. Unscrew the nut from the outer end of the brake cam and tap the cam out of the housing (**Figure 18**).

22. Unscrew nuts from the housing cover (**Figure 19**).

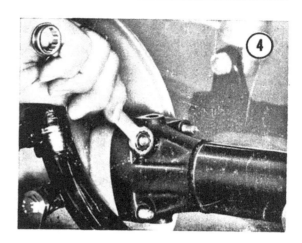

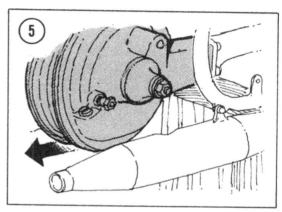

23. Install BMW tool No. 505 over the splines on the ring gear hub. Screw 2 Allen bolts into the threaded (size M 6) holes in the housing cover and press it off by turning the bolts clockwise (**Figure 20**).

24. Refer to **Figure 21**; remove the housing cover with the ring gear and the needle bearing inner race and shim.

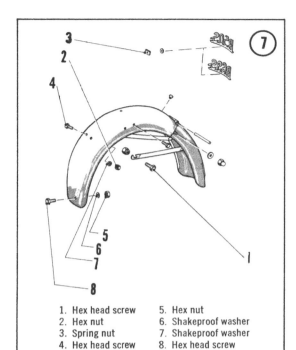

1. Hex head screw   5. Hex nut
2. Hex nut   6. Shakeproof washer
3. Spring nut   7. Shakeproof washer
4. Hex head screw   8. Hex head screw

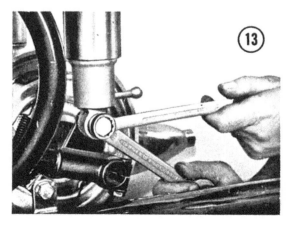

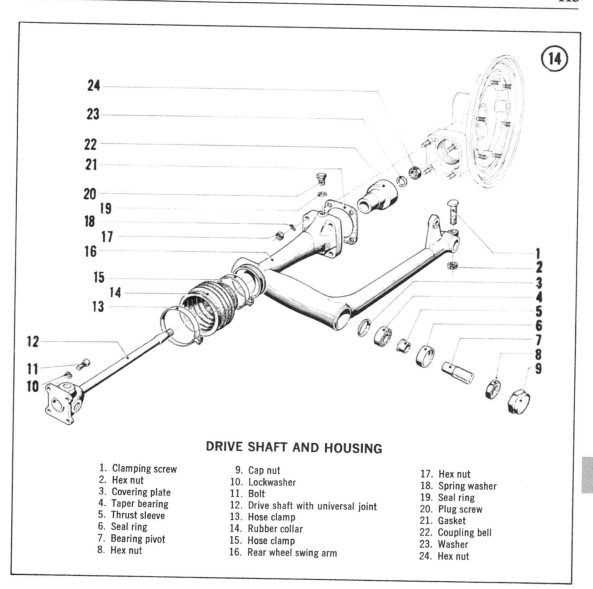

DRIVE SHAFT AND HOUSING

1. Clamping screw
2. Hex nut
3. Covering plate
4. Taper bearing
5. Thrust sleeve
6. Seal ring
7. Bearing pivot
8. Hex nut

9. Cap nut
10. Lockwasher
11. Bolt
12. Drive shaft with universal joint
13. Hose clamp
14. Rubber collar
15. Hose clamp
16. Rear wheel swing arm

17. Hex nut
18. Spring washer
19. Seal ring
20. Plug screw
21. Gasket
22. Coupling bell
23. Washer
24. Hex nut

10

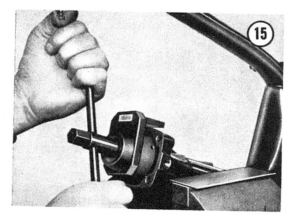

25. If the ball bearing assembly did not come out of the housing cover when it was pressed off, remove the large seal, heat the cover and tap it against a wood block to knock out the bearing. Then, remove the shim from behind the bearing.

26. Heat the main housing to 180°F and pull out the needle bearing outer race and the seal immediately behind it. Pull the inner race off the ring gear shaft.

27. The lock tab is behind the coupling hub nut in front of the housing. Bend lock tab down.

28. Install BMW tool No. 507 (or No. 256) over the swing arm mounting studs (**Figure 22**) and unscrew the nut with a 22mm socket. Remove nut, lock tab plate, and coupling hub.

29. Unscrew the threaded ring with BMW tool No. 560a and remove the ring and the spacer. Remove the seal from the threaded ring.

30. Heat the drive housing to 180°F, install a puller (BMW tool No. 259/1), and pull out the pinion with the ball bearing assembly. Pull the bearing off the shaft and remove the shim behind it.

31. Tap off the ball bearing assembly behind the ring gear. Use a soft metal drift inserted through the holes in the gear (**Figure 23**).

INSPECTION

1. Check all bearings, races, sleeves, seals, and the swing arm bearing pins for wear, pitting, and galling. Replace as necessary.

2. Check the ring gear and pinion for excessive wear and for chipped or broken teeth. If any of these conditions are present, the ring gear and pinion must be replaced as a set. The dash number (e.g., 314-10 or 314+10) indicates, in hundredths of a millimeter, the deviation from standard of the position of the pinion. This will be important during reassembly.

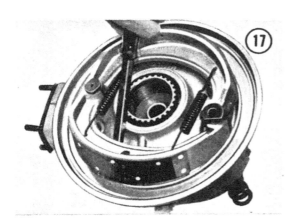

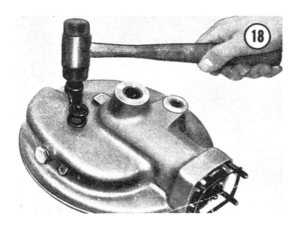

1. Sleeve (No. 505)   2. Allen bolts

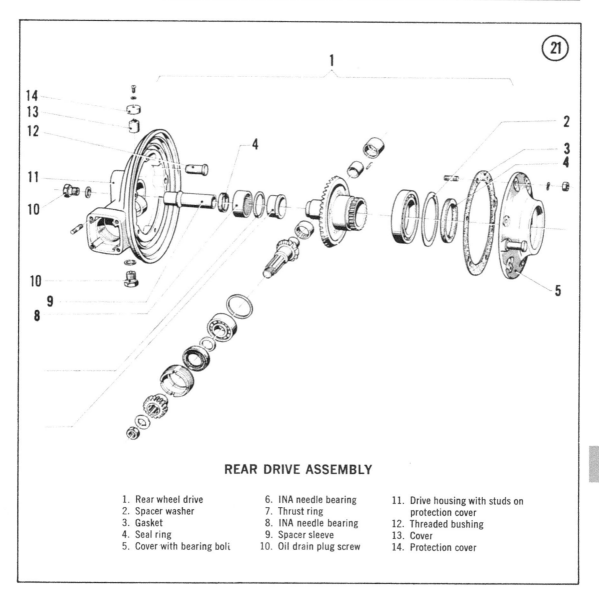

REAR DRIVE ASSEMBLY

1. Rear wheel drive
2. Spacer washer
3. Gasket
4. Seal ring
5. Cover with bearing bolt
6. INA needle bearing
7. Thrust ring
8. INA needle bearing
9. Spacer sleeve
10. Oil drain plug screw
11. Drive housing with studs on protection cover
12. Threaded bushing
13. Cover
14. Protection cover

10

3. With the gearset installed in the housing (see *Reassembly*), check the backlash. Install a dial indicator and BMW tool No. 5042 on the outer edge of the ring gear. Refer to **Figure 24**.

4. Grasp the drive splines and gently turn the gear from one extreme of free play to the other, without turning the pinion. Correct backlash is between 0.15 and 0.20mm (0.0059 -0.0079 in.).

5. Apply Prussian Blue dye to a tooth on the ring gear and rotate it to make contact with the pinion. Check the contact pattern on the tooth. If the contact pattern is in the center of the tooth or just slightly toward the forward end (**Figure 25**), the mesh of the gears is correct. If the contact pattern is at the forward end of the tooth (**Figure 26**), a thicker spacer is required between the pinion bearing and the housing (**Figure 27**). The backlash must be corrected by installing a thinner thrust washer between the ring gear and the needle bearing assembly (**Figure 28**). If the contact pattern is at the rear end of the tooth (**Figure 29**), a thinner spacer is required between the pinion bearing and the housing. The backlash must be corrected by installing a thicker thrust washer between the ring gear and the needle bearing assembly.

> NOTE: *Each time the pinion is removed and reinstalled, the housing must be heated to 180°F.*

6. Double check the backlash and mesh.
7. Check the end play of the ring gear. Place two equal prisms on the mating surface of the cover (**Figure 30**), check the distance with a height gauge, and write it down.

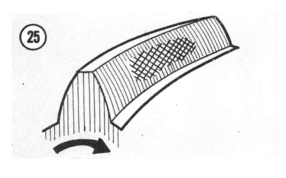

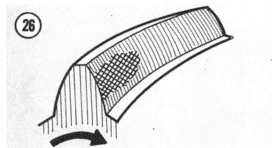

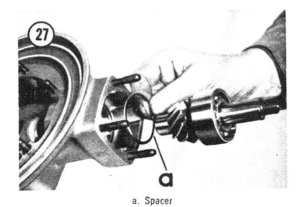

a. Spacer

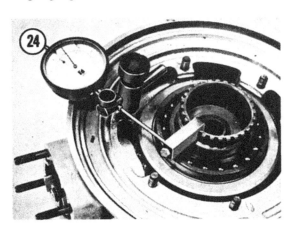

b. Thrust washer

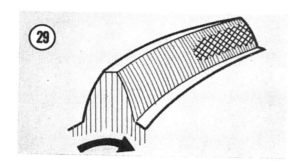

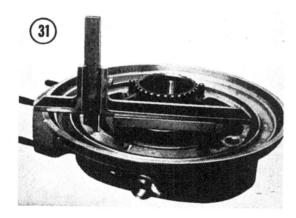

Recessed pin (arrow)

8. Install a gasket on the mating surface in the housing, place one of the prisms on the bearing (**Figure 31**), measure the distance with the height gauge, and write it down. Subtract the second measurement from the first, and then subtract the required side play 0.05mm (0.0020 in.) from the answer. The final result is the thickness of the thrust ring required.

NOTE: *Because the gasket compresses slightly during installation, it is advisable to use the next smaller ring if the computation indicates the correct one may possibly place the ring gear under pressure.*

REASSEMBLY

1. Heat the large ball bearing assembly for the ring gear to 180°F and reinstall it on the gear.

2. Heat the housing to 180°F and reinstall the needle bearing assembly at the rear of the pinion shaft. Replace the recessed pin (**Figure 32**) which holds the needle bearing in the housing.

3. See **Figure 33** and reinstall pinion and spacer.

4. Heat the housing and reinstall the ball bearing assembly on the pinion with the open side of the bearing facing forward. Apply gasket cement to the inside spacer and install it.

5. Press a new seal into the threaded ring with BMW tool No. 255 (**Figure 34**). Install the ring with BMW tool No. 506a or No. 253. Torque the ring to 10-11 mkg (72-87 ft.-lb.).

6. Reinstall the coupling hub, a new lock tab plate, and the nut. Place the locking fixture on the hub and torque the nut to 10-11 mkg (72-87 ft -lb.). Bend the lock tab to lock the nut

7. Install the seal in the housing with BMW tool No 258 (**Figure 35**).

8. Install the spacer and inner bearing race on ring gear with BMW tool No. 254 (**Figure 36**).

9. Heat the housing to 180°F, install the spacer, and press in the needle bearing with BMW tool No 257 (**Figure 37**).

10. Heat the cover to 180°F and press in the seal with BMW tool No 251 (**Figure 38**).

11. Heat the cover to 180°F, install the spacer, and press in the ball bearing.

10

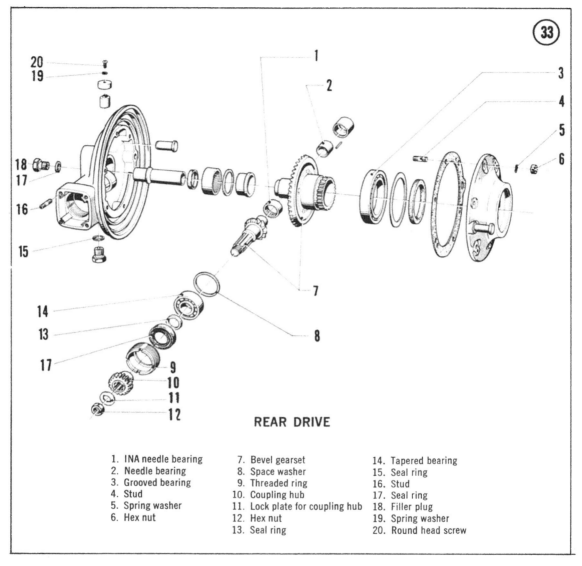

REAR DRIVE

1. INA needle bearing	7. Bevel gearset	14. Tapered bearing
2. Needle bearing	8. Space washer	15. Seal ring
3. Grooved bearing	9. Threaded ring	16. Stud
4. Stud	10. Coupling hub	17. Seal ring
5. Spring washer	11. Lock plate for coupling hub	18. Filler plug
6. Hex nut	12. Hex nut	19. Spring washer
	13. Seal ring	20. Round head screw

12. Install the ring gear in the housing and place a new gasket on the sealing surface.

13. Put the cover in place and heat it to 180°F. Put the sleeve (BMW tool No. 505) over the splines and carefully tap the cover down. Install the washers on the studs, screw on the nuts, and torque them to 1.8-2.1 mkg (13-14.2 ft.-lb.).

14. Reinstall the brake arm and brake shoes.

15. Degrease the conical end of the drive shaft (**Figure 39**) and insert it into the swing arm.

> NOTE: *On early models with a conicity of 1:5 on the drive shaft, the cone must be lapped in with a fine grade of grinding compound if either the shaft or coupling are replaced. On later models with a conicity of 1:6, this is not necessary. If either part is being replaced, check with your dealer to make sure both parts have the same conicity.*

16. Reinstall the coupling, screw on the nut, and torque it to 13-15 mkg (94-108 ft.-lb.) for US models.

> CAUTION
> *If there is a key groove in the coupling, it can be installed only on a shaft with a groove and a key. If there is no groove in the coupling, it can be installed on either a grooved or ungrooved shaft.*

17. Grease the swing arm pivot bearings and races. Reinstall the grease retainers, bearing races, bearings, thrust sleeves, and rubber seals in the swing arm.

18. Set the swing arm in place, between the pivot bosses on the main frame, and screw in the pivot pins, but do not tighten them.

19. Reinstall the lower end of the left spring/shock on the swing arm.

20. Position the swing arm so the clearance between the ends of the pivot tube and the pivot

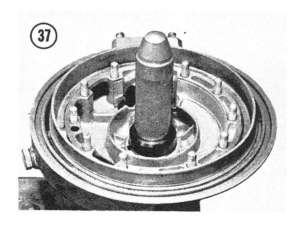

10

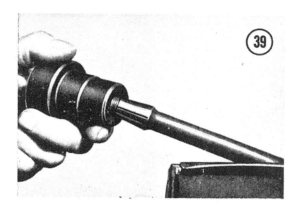

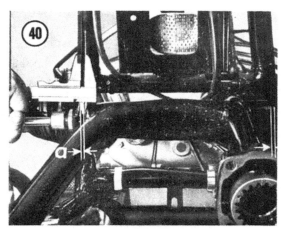

a-a. Clearance

bosses on the frame is the same on both sides (**Figure 40**).

21. Screw in the pivot pins while maintaining the clearance. When both pins are screwed in all the way, screw on the locknuts by hand. Tighten the pivot pins and then loosen them slightly to relieve the loading on the bearings. Hold the pins with a pin wrench and tighten the locknuts. Grease the bearings with a grease gun (**Figure 41**) and replace the cap nuts.

22. Check to make sure the clearance is equal on both sides and adjust if necessary.

23. The rest of the reassembly is in the reverse order of disassembly.

CHAPTER ELEVEN

WHEELS AND BRAKES

Front and rear wheels are identical. The wheel is shown in **Figures 1 and 2**.

WHEEL REMOVAL

Front Wheel

1. Place the motorcycle on its centerstand and set a block beneath the frame at the front of the engine to lift the front wheel off the ground (**Figure 3**).

2. Disconnect the brake anchor and cable.

3. Remove the axle nut, loosen the axle pinch bolts, and pull out the axle (**Figure 4**).

4. Remove the front wheel and brake assembly.

Rear Wheel

1. Place the motorcycle on its centerstand and set a block beneath the frame behind the engine to lift the rear wheel off the ground (**Figure 5**).

2. Unscrew the axle nut on right side. See **Figure 6**.

3. Place a drift pin into the hole in the left end of the axle and pull it out (**Figure 7**).

4. Pull the wheel to the left to clear the final drive and remove it to the rear. It may be necessary to lean the motorcycle to the left. It is a good idea to have some assistance with this task.

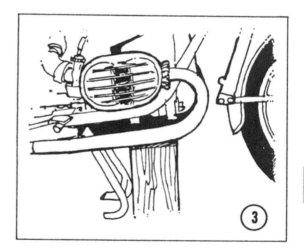

1. Axle nut   2. Pinch bolt   3. Axle

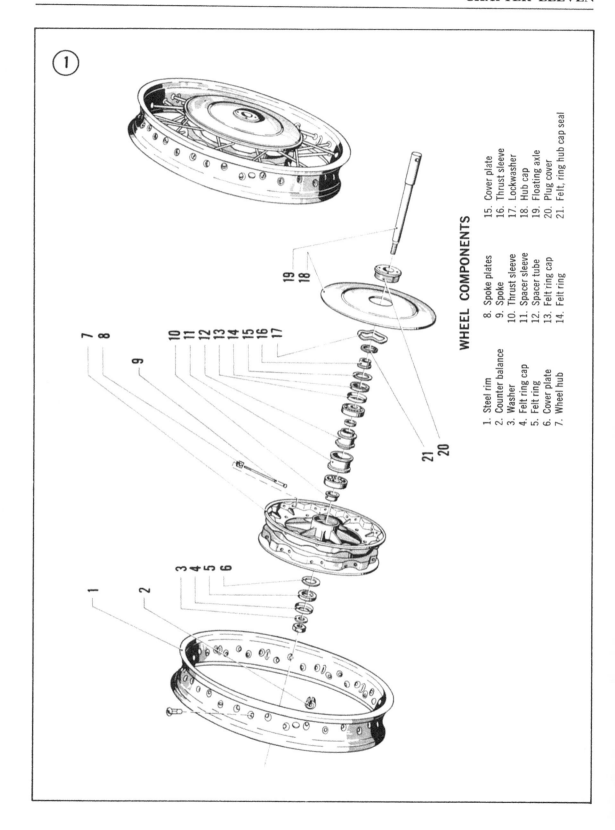

WHEEL COMPONENTS

1. Steel rim
2. Counter balance
3. Washer
4. Felt ring cap
5. Felt ring
6. Cover plate
7. Wheel hub
8. Spoke plates
9. Spoke
10. Thrust sleeve
11. Spacer sleeve
12. Spacer tube
13. Felt ring cap
14. Felt ring
15. Cover plate
16. Thrust sleeve
17. Lockwasher
18. Hub cap
19. Floating axle
20. Plug cover
21. Felt, ring hub cap seal

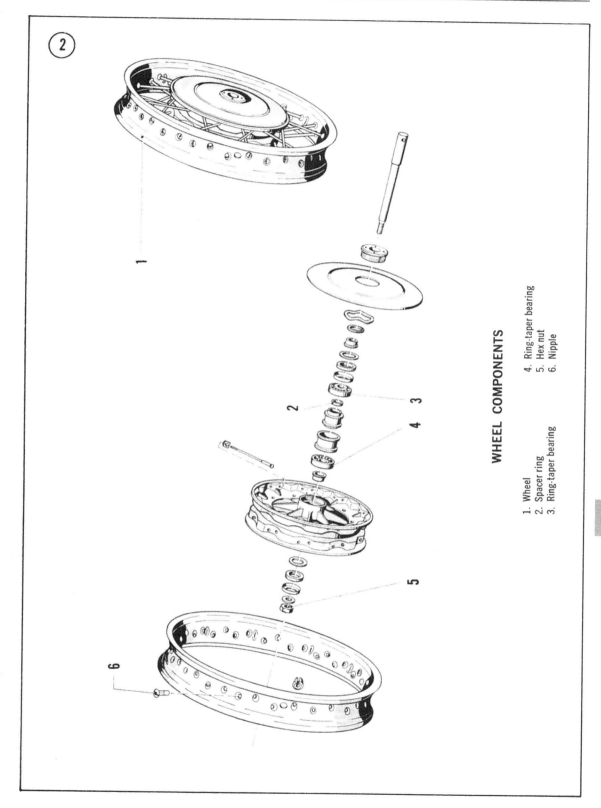

WHEEL COMPONENTS

1. Wheel
2. Spacer ring
3. Ring-taper bearing
4. Ring-taper bearing
5. Hex nut
6. Nipple

3. Pinch bolt

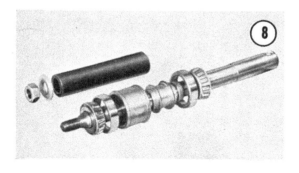

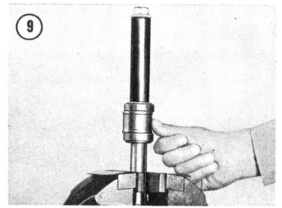

BEARINGS

The wheels have a tapered roller bearing assembly on each side of the wheel.

Removal

1. Remove the left side hub cap. The plug cover must be removed with a pin wrench.

2. Remove the washers, seals, spacers, and inner bearing races from each side of the wheel.

3. Remove the left side bearing assembly.

4. Working from the brake side of the hub, insert a drift (BMW tool No. 5078) into spacer sleeve. Tap out the left bearing outer race, outer spacer bushing, the right side bearing assembly, and spacer sleeve.

Inspection

1. Install the complete bearing set on the axle (**Figure 8**).

2. Using jaw protectors, clamp the axle in a vise and install a spacer sleeve over the axle. Secure it with the axle nut and washer.

> NOTE: *The spacer can be made of tubing which is about 20mm (0.787 in.) inside diameter and 120mm (4.72 in.) long.*

3. With the bearing assembly clamped firmly, there should be no apparent play, and the large spacer should be able to be displaced with moderate pressure (**Figure 9**). If the play is excessive or insufficient, replace the left side spacer with one of different size, as appropriate, to correct the clearance.

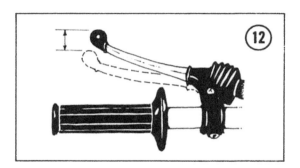

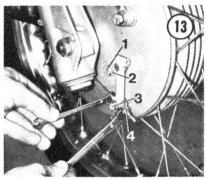

1. Adjustment cam   3. Arm
2. Lock nut   4. Cable adjustment nut

Installation

1. Heat the hub to about 200°F and tap in the outer bearing races with an installer (BMW tool No. 5080).

> NOTE: *The reducer bushing must be installed in the front wheel.*

2. Repack the bearings with about 10 grams of bearing grease.

3. Reassemble the remainder of the components in reverse order of disassembly.

SPOKE REPLACEMENT AND ADJUSTMENT

Spoke replacement and adjustment and wheel truing are jobs for an expert.

WHEEL BALANCING

The instructions presented cover static balancing. Dynamic balancing requires the use of a special machine.

1. Raise the wheel being balanced off the ground and rotate it.

2. When the wheel comes to rest, attach a weight to the spoke at the top of the wheel. Weights are available in 10 gram and 15 gram sizes, for either the 3.5mm (0.1378 in.) or 4mm (0.1575 in.) spokes.

3. Experiment with the weights until the wheel does not come to rest at the same point each time it is spun.

DRUM BRAKES

The front brake is a double-leading shoe design, and the rear brake is a single-leading shoe type. Brakes are shown in **Figures 10 and 11**.

Front Brake Disassembly

1. Remove the front wheel as outlined earlier in this chapter.

2. With a pair of pliers, unhook the springs from the brake shoes and remove them.

Brake Inspection

1. Check the braking surface of the drum. If it is excessively worn or grooved, it will have to be turned down on a lathe. This should be a job for an expert.

2. Check the brake lining for wear and remove foreign matter with a wire brush. If the linings are worn to a point where the rivets will soon come in contact with the drum, replace the linings.

Front Brake Reassembly

Reassemble the brakes and reinstall them and the wheels in reverse order of disassembly.

Front Brake Adjustment

1. Adjust play in hand lever to between 8mm and 15mm (0.315 and 0.591 in.). Refer to **Figure 12**.

2. Refer to **Figure 13** and loosen the locknut on the adjustment cam. With an Allen wrench, turn the adjustment cam counterclockwise until it is tight. Then, turn it clockwise until the lower front brake lever has 4mm (0.157 in.) free movement (measured at the cable anchor) before the shoe contacts the drum.

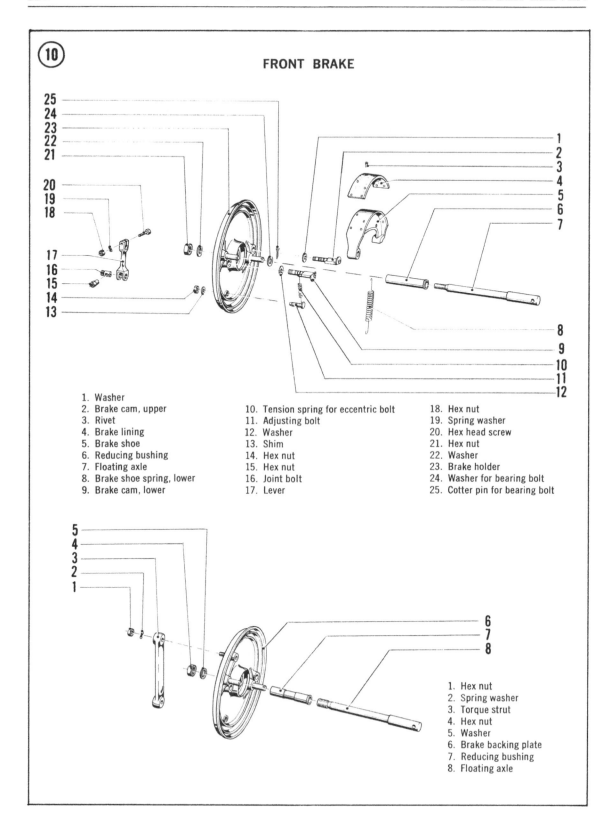

⑩   **FRONT BRAKE**

25
24
23
22
21

20
19
18

17
16
15
14
13

1
2
3
4
5
6
7

8
9
10
11
12

1. Washer
2. Brake cam, upper
3. Rivet
4. Brake lining
5. Brake shoe
6. Reducing bushing
7. Floating axle
8. Brake shoe spring, lower
9. Brake cam, lower

10. Tension spring for eccentric bolt
11. Adjusting bolt
12. Washer
13. Shim
14. Hex nut
15. Hex nut
16. Joint bolt
17. Lever

18. Hex nut
19. Spring washer
20. Hex head screw
21. Hex nut
22. Washer
23. Brake holder
24. Washer for bearing bolt
25. Cotter pin for bearing bolt

5
4
3
2
1

6
7
8

1. Hex nut
2. Spring washer
3. Torque strut
4. Hex nut
5. Washer
6. Brake backing plate
7. Reducing bushing
8. Floating axle

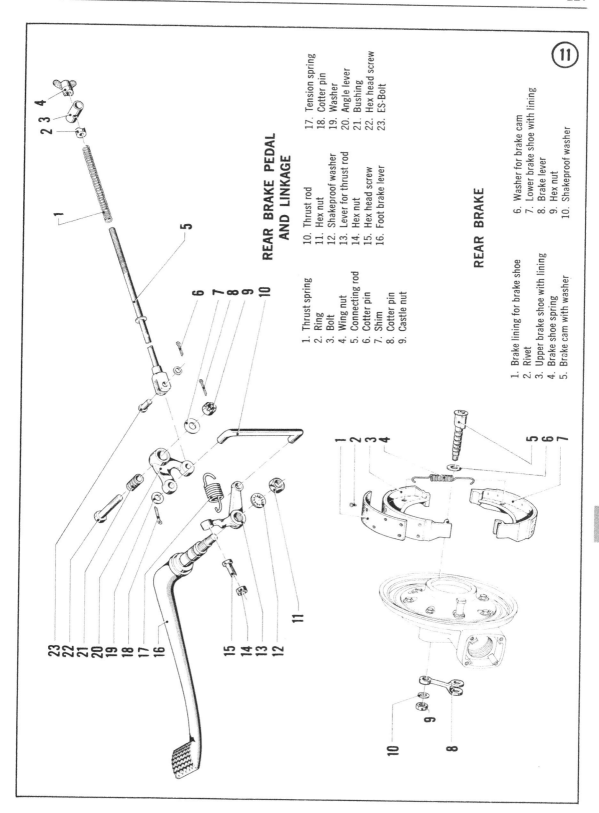

REAR BRAKE PEDAL AND LINKAGE

1. Thrust spring
2. Ring
3. Bolt
4. Wing nut
5. Connecting rod
6. Cotter pin
7. Shim
8. Cotter pin
9. Castle nut
10. Thrust rod
11. Hex nut
12. Shakeproof washer
13. Lever for thrust rod
14. Hex nut
15. Hex head screw
16. Foot brake lever
17. Tension spring
18. Cotter pin
19. Washer
20. Angle lever
21. Bushing
22. Hex head screw
23. ES-Bolt

REAR BRAKE

1. Brake lining for brake shoe
2. Rivet
3. Upper brake shoe with lining
4. Brake shoe spring
5. Brake cam with washer
6. Washer for brake cam
7. Lower brake shoe with lining
8. Brake lever
9. Hex nut
10. Shakeproof washer

3. Hold the cable sleeve at the rear of the lower brake arm with a 4mm wrench and turn the 10mm adjuster nut until the free movement of the upper brake arm is 4mm (0.157 in.) before the shoe contacts the drum.

Rear Brake Adjustment

1. Turn the wing nut on the end of the rear brake rod (**Figure 14**) clockwise until the brake shoes drag in the drum.

2. Back off the wing nut three to five turns.

CAUTION

Too little free movement in the brake controls can cause the brakes to lock during application.

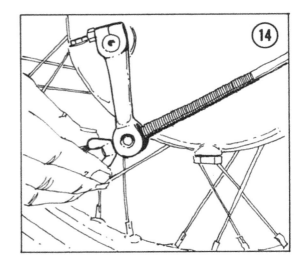

CHAPTER TWELVE

FRAME

Frame service is limited to inspection for cracks in welds and tubes. If bending damage is suspected or apparent, the frame should be inspected and repaired as necessary by an authorized BMW service shop.

STRIPPING THE FRAME

Refer to the appropriate chapters and remove the engine, transmission, controls, electrical system, seat, fuel tank, wheels, and suspension.

Figures 1 through 3 are provided as general reference for the frame and removal/installation of related components.

REASSEMBLY

Reassembly of the frame and installation of major components should follow reverse order of disassembly.

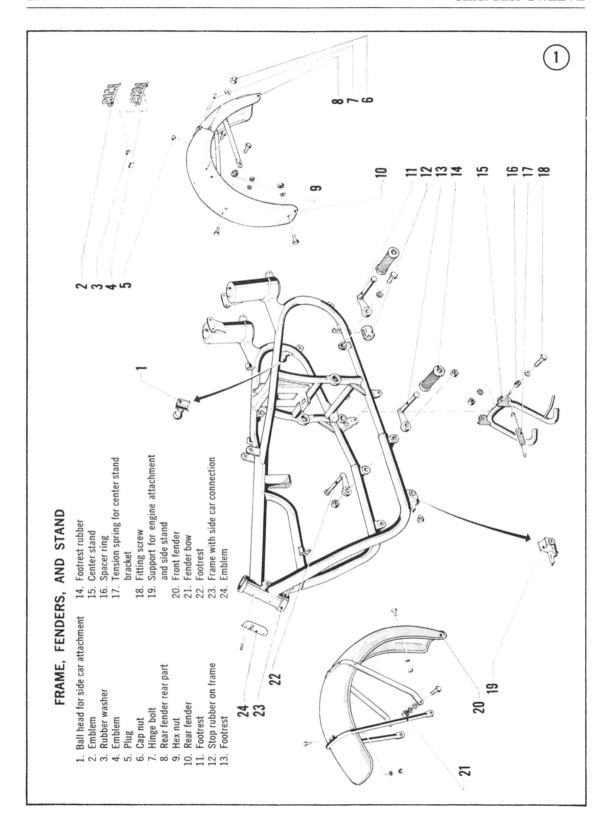

FRAME, FENDERS, AND STAND

1. Ball head for side car attachment
2. Emblem
3. Rubber washer
4. Emblem
5. Plug
6. Cap nut
7. Hinge bolt
8. Rear fender rear part
9. Hex nut
10. Rear fender
11. Footrest
12. Stop rubber on frame
13. Footrest
14. Footrest rubber
15. Center stand
16. Spacer ring
17. Tension spring for center stand bracket
18. Fitting screw
19. Support for engine attachment and side stand
20. Front fender
21. Fender bow
22. Footrest
23. Frame with side car connection
24. Emblem

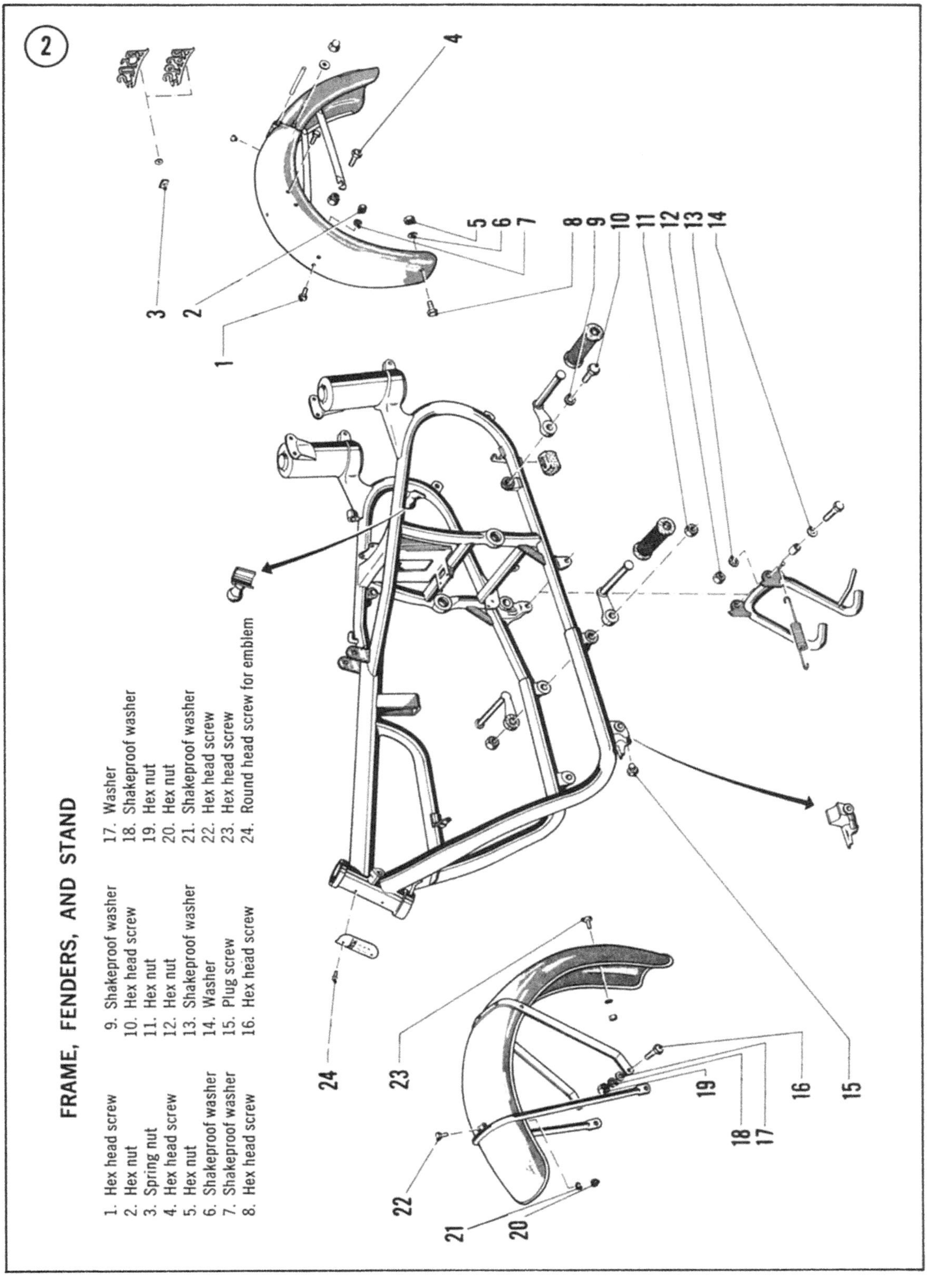

FRAME, FENDERS, AND STAND

1. Hex head screw
2. Hex nut
3. Spring nut
4. Hex head screw
5. Hex nut
6. Shakeproof washer
7. Shakeproof washer
8. Hex head screw
9. Shakeproof washer
10. Hex head screw
11. Hex nut
12. Hex nut
13. Shakeproof washer
14. Washer
15. Plug screw
16. Hex head screw
17. Washer
18. Shakeproof washer
19. Hex nut
20. Hex nut
21. Shakeproof washer
22. Hex head screw
23. Hex head screw
24. Round head screw for emblem

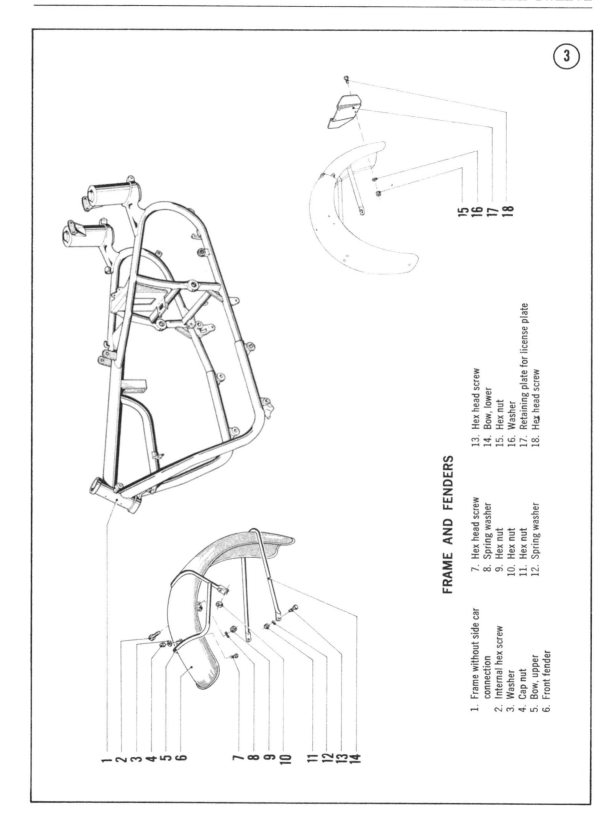

FRAME AND FENDERS

1. Frame without side car connection
2. Internal hex screw
3. Washer
4. Cap nut
5. Bow, upper
6. Front fender
7. Hex head screw
8. Spring washer
9. Hex nut
10. Hex nut
11. Hex nut
12. Spring washer
13. Hex head screw
14. Bow, lower
15. Hex nut
16. Washer
17. Retaining plate for license plate
18. Hex head screw

CHAPTER THIRTEEN

LIGHTING, WIRING, AND INSTRUMENTS

Lighting equipment, horn, control switches, wiring harnesses, and instruments are covered in this chapter.

HEADLIGHT

Refer to **Figure 1** for construction of the headlight.

Disassembly/Assembly

1. Loosen the screw at the bottom of the headlight rim and remove the rim, lens, and reflector.
2. Remove the bulb holder from the reflector (**Figure 2**).
3. Remove the bulb from the holder by pushing in, turning it counterclockwise, and pulling out.
4. Perform *Inspection* procedure, then assemble by reversing this procedure.

Inspection

1. Visually check the bulb for broken filaments and replace it if necessary.
2. Check the wiring for frayed insulation and corrosion of the plugs and terminals.

Adjustment

Refer to **Figure 3**.
1. Check the tire pressure (**Table 1**) for solo

Table 1	TIRE PRESSURE
Front	Rear
1.75 kg-cm² (24 psi)	1.8 kg-cm² (26 psi)

operation and adjust it if necessary.
2. Set the adjusters on the rear spring/shock absorbers in the SOLO position.
3. Place the motorcycle perpendicular to a light-colored wall, at a distance of 16.5 feet (5 meters), measured from the wall to the headlight lens.
4. Slightly loosen the mounting bolts on either side of the headlight body.
5. With the motorcycle on its wheels, mount it and have someone measure the distance from the center of the headlight lens to the ground.
6. Mark a cross on the wall at the same distance from the ground.

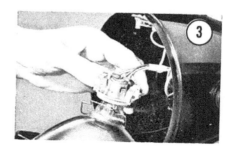

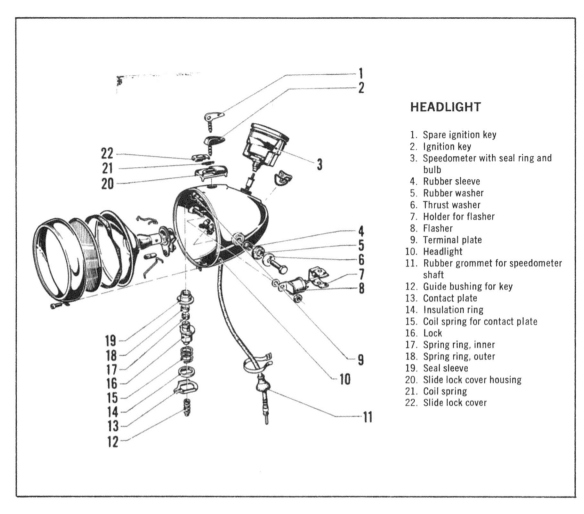

HEADLIGHT

1. Spare ignition key
2. Ignition key
3. Speedometer with seal ring and bulb
4. Rubber sleeve
5. Rubber washer
6. Thrust washer
7. Holder for flasher
8. Flasher
9. Terminal plate
10. Headlight
11. Rubber grommet for speedometer shaft
12. Guide bushing for key
13. Contact plate
14. Insulation ring
15. Coil spring for contact plate
16. Lock
17. Spring ring, inner
18. Spring ring, outer
19. Seal sleeve
20. Slide lock cover housing
21. Coil spring
22. Slide lock cover

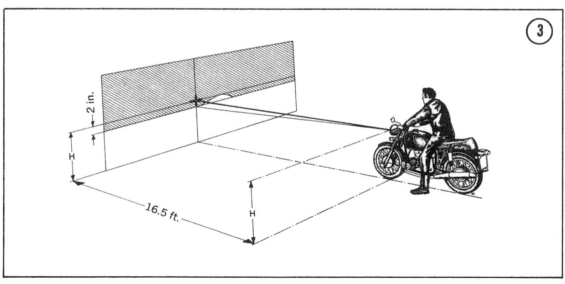

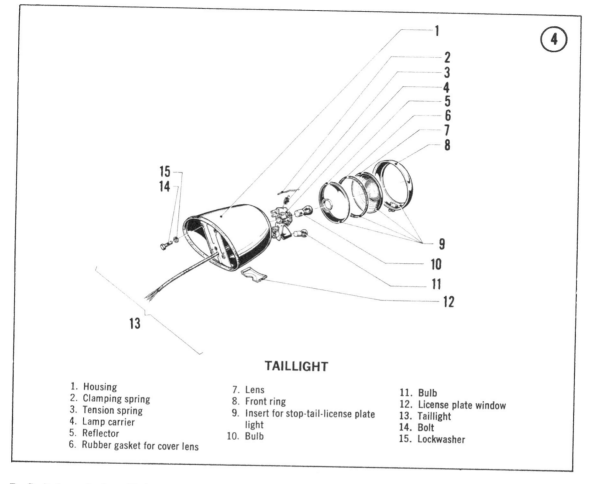

TAILLIGHT

1. Housing
2. Clamping spring
3. Tension spring
4. Lamp carrier
5. Reflector
6. Rubber gasket for cover lens

7. Lens
8. Front ring
9. Insert for stop-tail-license plate light
10. Bulb

11. Bulb
12. License plate window
13. Taillight
14. Bolt
15. Lockwasher

7. Switch on the headlight and select high beam. Align the headlight so that the cross is in the center of the illuminated area.

8. Select low beam. The upper edge of the illuminated area should be 2 in. (5 cm) below the cross, rising to the left where, at its apex, it meets the horizontal line of the cross.

9. When the adjustment is correct, tighten the headlight mounting bolts.

TAIL/STOPLIGHTS

Refer to **Figure 4** for construction of the taillight/stoplight.

Disassembly/Assembly

1. Undo the screw at the bottom of the light rim and remove the rim, reflector, and bulb holder (**Figure 5**).

2. Remove the bulbs from their sockets by pushing in, turning counterclockwise, and pulling out.

3. Perform *Inspection* procedure, then assemble by reversing this procedure.

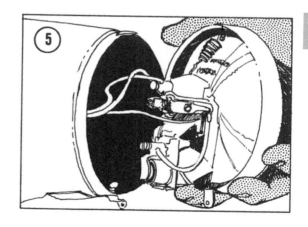

13

Inspection

1. Visually check the bulbs for broken filaments and replace them if necessary.

2. Check the wiring for frayed insulation and corrosion of the plugs and connections.

TURN SIGNALS

Refer to **Figure 6** for construction of the turn signals.

Removal

1. Remove the 2 screws from the lens and remove the lens.

2. Remove the bulb from its socket by pushing in, turning counterclockwise, and pulling out.

Inspection

1. Visually check the bulb for broken filament and replace it if necessary.

2. Check the wiring for frayed insulation and corrosion of the terminals.

FLASHER RELAY

Refer to **Figure 7** for identification of the flasher relay. In both models, the relay is located inside the headlight body.

Disassembly/Assembly

1. Remove the headlight lens and reflector as described earlier.

2. Unscrew the nut holding the relay (**Figure 8**) in place, pull out the relay, and unplug the leads. Note their locations for reinstallation.

3. Assembly is the reverse of this procedure.

Inspection

1. Flasher rate should be between 65 and 90 times per minute. If the rate is abnormal, check the ratings on the signal bulbs; the flashing rate is affected by the resistance of the bulbs.

2. Check for frayed wiring insulation and corroded terminals.

3. If the wiring and connections are sound, and if the bulb ratings are correct and the flasher still does not operate normally, replace it.

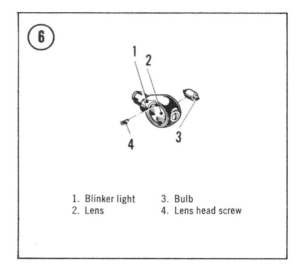

1. Blinker light   3. Bulb
2. Lens   4. Lens head screw

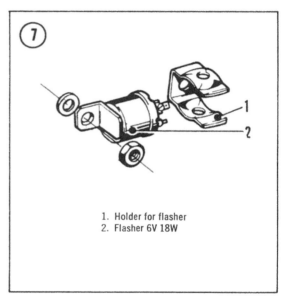

1. Holder for flasher
2. Flasher 6V 18W

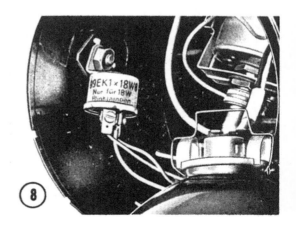

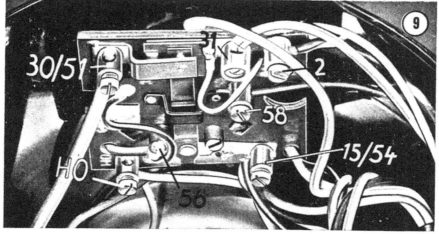

1. Ignition only
2. Ignition and headlight
3. Ignition and parking lights

IGNITION SWITCH

Refer to **Figure 9** for construction of the ignition switch. On all models, the switch is located inside the headlight body.

Disassembly

1. Remove the headlight lens and reflector as described earlier.

2. Disconnect the battery ground lead.

3. Assembly is the reverse of this procedure.

Inspection

1. Check the switch terminals for tightness and corrosion. Check wiring for frayed insulation.

2. Refer to the wiring diagrams at the end of the chapter. Check the continuity of the switch, in each of the 3 operating positions (**Figure 10**), with a bench tester. If the test lamp lights, the circuit is good. If it does not, the circuit is open and the switch must be repaired or replaced.

SWITCHES

Service on dimmer, turn signal, horn, and starter switches is limited to continuity checks in the appropriate circuits.

1. Check the terminals of the switch being tested for tightness and for corrosion of the contacts. Check the wiring for frayed insulation.

2. Refer to wiring diagrams at the end of the chapter. Check the continuity of each switch, in its operating position, with a bench tester. If the test lamp lights, the circuit is good. If it does not, the circuit is open and the switch must be repaired or replaced.

HORN

Service on the horn is limited to checking continuity (see above), increasing or decreasing the volume, and cleaning contacts inside the horn.

1. To adjust the volume of the horn, turn the adjuster screw in to increase it or out to decrease it.

2. If switch and wiring continuity are good and the horn will not sound, disconnect the leads

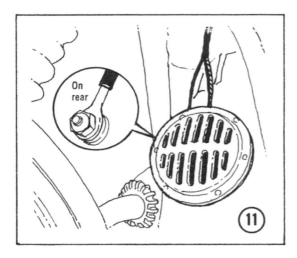

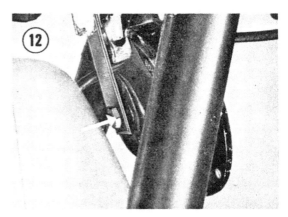

(**Figure 11**), unscrew the bolt (**Figure 12**), and remove the horn.

3. Unscrew the screws from the horn face and remove it.

4. Dress the contacts with a point file or Flexstone, reassemble horn, and adjust its volume.

FRONT BRAKE LIGHT SWITCH

1. Check the continuity of the switch and inspect the wiring for frayed insulation and corroded contacts.

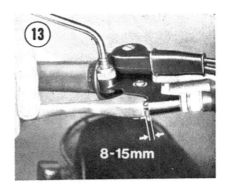

2. With the brake lever free play correctly adjusted (**Figure 13**), rotate the switch adjuster located behind the cable adjuster. The brake lamp should light when about one-half of the free play is taken up.

REAR BRAKE LIGHT SWITCH

1. Check the continuity of the switch and inspect the wiring for frayed insulation and corroded contacts.

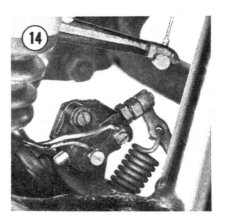

2. With the brake pedal adjusted in accordance with the instructions in Chapter Ten, loosen the locknut on the adjuster bolt (**Figure 14**). Rotate the adjuster so that the brake lamp lights when about one-half of the free play is taken up. Retighten the locknut.

NEUTRAL SWITCH

Servicing of the neutral indicator switch is covered in Chapter Five, *Reassembly.*

INDICATOR LIGHTS

Indicator and warning lights have bayonet-type bases. Their service is limited to continuity checks, visual inspection for broken filaments, and replacement. The bulbs are located in plug-in sockets inside the headlight body.

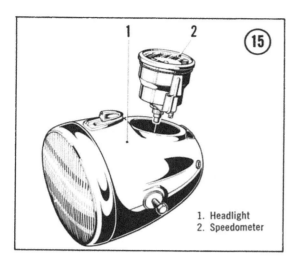

1. Headlight
2. Speedometer

INSTRUMENTS

The speedometer is cable driven. Repairs should be made only by an expert. The instrument is shown in **Figure 15**.

Disassembly

1. Remove the headlight ring, lens, and reflector as outlined earlier.

2. Disconnect the cables from the rear of the instrument.

3. Carefully push the speedometer upward and out of the headlight body.

WIRING HARNESS

The wiring harness is color coded in accordance with wiring diagrams. Continuity checks can be conducted with the harness installed; it should be removed and replaced only if insulation is frayed or burned. To remove harness, first remove fuel tank, seat, and light lenses. Unscrew and unplug harness leads from electrical components, unfasten harness straps, and remove harness. Reinstall the new harness in reverse order of disassembly.

WIRING DIAGRAM

1. Blinker — horn switch
2. Flasher unit
3. Double filament bulb
4. Parking light
5. Dimmer and headlight flasher switch
6. Right blinker
7. Cable connector (2-pole)
8. Ignition and light switch
9. Left blinker
10. Neutral indicator
11. Charging indicator
12. Speedometer lights
13. Horn
14. Ignition magneto
15. Spark plug adaptor with interference suppression
16. Electrical jack (socket)
17. Cable connector (3-pole)
18. Stoplight switch
19. Generator
20. Stop and taillight
21. License plate light
22. Neutral indicator contact
23. Battery

Sidecar
24. Front side light
25. Blinker
26. Cable connector (1-pole)
27. Rear side light

Wiring Color Code
BL = Blue
BR = Brown
GE = Yellow
GN = Green
GR = Gray
RT = Red
SW = Black
VI = Violet
WS = White

Example:
0.75 BR = 0.75 sq.mm, brown.

CHAPTER FOURTEEN

RESTORATION

The pre-1970 models built BMW's reputation for quality and longevity. Many of these bikes have logged impressive mileage, and are still in daily use—some by the original owners. But time and mileage eventually take their toll, and even these solid bikes need freshening occasionally.

A ground-up restoration is not always desirable. Total restoration can be very expensive, time-consuming, and require hours of skilled workmanship. A clean, but unrestored bike, may even be more valuable to some collectors. The information in this chapter will help you restore most of the bike's original appearance and performance, and certainly restore your pride in owning one of the world's best vehicles.

ORIGINAL PAINT RESTORATION

If the original paint is in reasonably good condition, it can be restored by "compounding" and waxing.

Start by obtaining a bottle of touch-up paint from your dealer to match the original paint. If your dealer cannot obtain the proper match, you can get aftermarket brands such as Krylon, Lubritech, or Dupli-Color from any automotive supply store. Use the brush included with the paint and dab it on any nicks or small scratches. Larger areas should be sanded smooth and touched up with spray paint, also available from the same sources as the bottle-type.

After the paint has had time to dry, rub out the painted areas with 3-M or DuPont rubbing compound and a dampened piece of terry cloth. Follow the directions on the can for best results.

Follow the compounding by dry buffing the painted areas with a piece of clean terry cloth. Finish off with a good brand (DuPont, Turtle-Wax, etc.) of cleaner/paste wax.

To achieve a better-than-new finish, you can also apply a coat of Armor-All or Meguiar's silicone glaze. Again, follow the manufacturer's directions to achieve the best results.

REPAINTING

Paint which is badly scratched or deteriorated will not be salvageable and you should start from scratch. **Figure 1** shows many of the original paint and pin striping schemes used. It is possible to obtain an excellent paint job with aerosol spray cans even if you have never attempted this type of work before.

If you do not wish to paint the bike yourself, you can save a lot of money by removing all the parts to be painted and preparing them properly for paint. Now would be a good time for a custom paint job, so consider it while you have the chance.

Remove all pieces from the bike that will be painted one color, such as the gas tank, fenders, headlight housing, and side covers. Various parts of this manual will tell you how. You may also want to install a fairing and other accessories, so buy them now and have everything

①

R51/2 (1950)
500cc OHV

R51/3 (1951-1954)
500cc OHV

R50 (1955)
500cc OHV

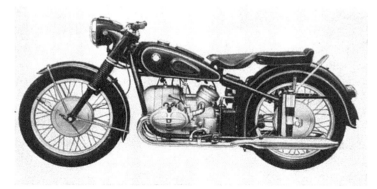

R68 (1952-1954)
600cc OHV

R69 (1955)
600cc OHV

R67/2 (1952-1954) 600cc OHV
R67/3 (1955) 600cc OHV

R60 (1956)
600cc OHV

14

painted at once to save money and assure a paint match.

The original paint will probably make a good primer coat for the new paint if it is properly cleaned and sanded first. Most automotive stores carry "paint pre-cleaner" just for this purpose. This will remove any wax and imbedded silicones from the paint. This is essential or the new paint will develop "chicken feet," crazing marks, and craters.

After the pre-cleaner, clean the painted parts with a solution of warm water and scouring cleanser. Be sure to rinse the paint well with clean water to remove any soapy residue. While the paint is still wet, sand the entire surface with No. 600 grit wet-and-dry sandpaper to achieve an obviously rough surface. This will give the new paint a surface with a "tooth" to hang onto. Otherwise, the old paint may be too smooth and will shed the new paint. Set everything aside to dry for at least eight hours.

After eight hours, apply masking tape to everything which does not get painted. This includes any chrome trim which cannot be removed. On most of the BMW's, you can remove everything, including fuel petcocks, trim, badges, etc. You are now ready to paint the parts or take them to a paint shop.

If you paint the parts yourself, be sure to use a good quality brand such as Krylon, Dupli-Color, or Lubritech. Cheap paints will only cause trouble. Follow the instructions on the cans for best results and paint only on warm, dry days. Never paint on a rainy or foggy day.

If the paint comes out less than perfect, do not worry. Paint which is "orange peel" (rough and wavy) can be compounded as described under *Original Paint Restoration*. Runs can be removed by lightly sanding with No. 400 wet-and-dry sandpaper followed by compounding and waxing. The areas being painted are so small and separated from other painted areas that the discoloration or mistakes will not appear as bad. Do not attempt any of these repairs until the paint has had several days to cure.

UPHOLSTERY

There are several companies who make seat slipcovers that simply tie onto the original seat

in less than a minute. These are excellent to hide tears, rips, or discoloration. They also have the advantage of costing far less than a professional reupholstery job.

If the seat is badly damaged, have it restored by a specialist.

CHROMED PARTS

One of the first areas to deteriorate on any motorcycle is the chrome. You could buy all new parts to replace the old ones but these would deteriorate quickly too and the cost would be prohibitive. Instead, remove all the plated parts and take them to a metal finisher for replating. There are several different grades of chrome plate, so ask questions instead of just requesting chrome plating. The best type is triple-plating, preceded by buffing. You may prefer to have the parts nickel-plated to resist corrosion and pitting in areas near large bodies of water. The plater will generally give you a cost break on several parts done at the same time.

Chrome or stainless steel which has not completely corroded can be salvaged by cleaning with very fine steel wool and chrome cleaner. Be sure to apply wax and WD-40 or Armor-All after this treatment to retard further corrosion.

RUBBER OR VINYL PARTS

Any rubber parts which have ozone or age cracks should be replaced. BMW dealers will have most parts in stock, and can order the others for you. However, if the original parts appear salvageable, clean them with very fine steel wool and scouring powder. Apply a thin coat of Armor-All or silicone to preserve the rubber and renew its appearance. Tires can be made to look brand new this way.

PERFORMANCE

The other chapters of this manual explain how to restore the bike to its original condition mechanically. Very little has been done to increase performance, though. If this is your interest, you are better advised to keep your pre-70 stock, and buy a later model for performance.

APPENDIX

SPECIFICATIONS

SPECIFICATIONS, MODEL R 50 US

DIMENSIONS	
Overall length	84 in.
Overall width	26 in.
Overall height	39.2 in.
Wheelbase	56.3 in.
Road clearance	5.9 in.
Tire size: front	3.50 x 18
rear	4.00 x 18
WEIGHT	
Curb weight	430 lbs.
PERFORMANCE	
Maximum output	26 bhp at 5,800 rpm
Maximum torque	N. A.
Maximum speed	87 mph
Acceleration (0 to 60)	10 sec.
ENGINE	
Type	4-stroke
Displacement	493cc
Bore x stroke	68mm x 68mm
Cylinders	Two, opposed
Compression ratio	7.5:1
Starter	Kick lever

(continued)

SPECIFICATIONS, MODEL R 50 US (continued)

FUEL SYSTEM

Carburetors (2)	Bing, 1/24
Fuel tank capacity	4.5 gal.

LUBRICATION

Engine	Pressure, wet sump
Oil capacity	4.25 pts.
Gearbox	1.7 pts.

IGNITION SYSTEM

Ignition	Magneto
Ignition timing	9° BTC
Spark plugs	Bosch W 240 T1

ELECTRICAL EQUIPMENT

Generator	Shunt type
Battery	6 V, 16 AH
Headlight	6 V, 35W/35W
Tail/brake lamp	6 V, 5W/18W
Turn signal lamps	6 V, 18W
Neutral indicator lamp	6 V, 2W
Speedometer lamp	6 V, 0.6W
High beam indicator lamp	12 V, 2W
Turn signal indicator lamp	6 V, 2W

TRANSMISSION SYSTEM

Clutch	Dry, single plate with diaphragm spring
Transmission gears	4-speed, constant mesh
Gear shifting	Left foot, lever-operated, return change
Final reduction ratio	3.375:1
Transmission gear ratios	
1st	4.171:1
2nd	2.725:1
3rd	1.938:1
4th	1.54:1
Overall reduction ratio	
1st	14.08:1
2nd	9.20:1
3rd	6.54:1
4th	5.20:1

SUSPENSION

Front suspension	Hydraulically dampened leading-link fork
Rear suspension	Swing arm with hydraulically dampened three-way adjustable units

BRAKES

Front brake	Internal expanding, double-leading shoe
Rear brake	Internal expanding, single-leading shoe

SPECIFICATIONS, MODEL R 60 US

DIMENSIONS

Overall length	84 in.
Overall width	26 in.
Overall height	39.2 in.
Wheelbase	56.3 in.
Road clearance	5.9 in.
Tire size: front	3.50 x 18
rear	4.00 x 18

WEIGHT

Curb weight	430 lbs.

PERFORMANCE

Maximum output	30 bhp at 5,800 rpm
Maximum torque	N. A.
Maximum speed	90 mph
Acceleration (0 to 60)	8.5 sec.

ENGINE

Type	4-stroke
Displacement	593cc
Bore x stroke	72mm x 73mm
Cylinders	Two, opposed
Compression ratio	7.5:1
Starter	Kick lever

FUEL SYSTEM

Carburetors (2)	Bing, 1/24
Fuel tank capacity	4.5 gal.

LUBRICATION

Engine	Pressure, wet sump
Oil capacity	4.25 pts.
Gearbox	1.7 pts.

IGNITION SYSTEM

Ignition	Magneto
Ignition timing	9° BTC
Spark plugs	Bosch W 240 T1

ELECTRICAL EQUIPMENT

Generator	Shunt type
Battery	6 V, 16 AH
Headlight	6 V, 35W/35W
Tail/brake lamp	6 V, 5W/18W
Turn signal lamps	6 V, 18W
Neutral indicator lamp	6 V, 2W
Speedometer lamp	6 V, 0.6W
High beam indicator lamp	12 V, 2W
Turn signal indicator lamp	6 V, 2W

(continued)

15

SPECIFICATIONS, MODEL R 60 US (continued)

TRANSMISSION SYSTEM

Clutch	Dry, single plate with diaphragm spring
Transmission gears	4-speed, constant mesh
Gear shifting	Left foot, lever-operated, return change
Final reduction ratio	3.375:1

Transmission gear ratios

1st	4.171:1
2nd	2.725:1
3rd	1.938:1
4th	1.54:1

Overall reduction ratio

1st	14.08:1
2nd	9.20:1
3rd	6.54:1
4th	5.20:1

SUSPENSION

Front suspension	Hydraulically dampened leading-link fork
Rear suspension	Swing arm with hydraulically dampened three-way adjustable units

BRAKES

Front brake	Internal expanding, double-leading shoe
Rear brake	Internal expanding, single-leading shoe

SPECIFICATIONS, MODEL R 69 US

DIMENSIONS

Overall length	84 in.
Overall width	26 in.
Overall height	39.2 in.
Wheelbase	56.3 in.
Road clearance	5.9 in.
Tire size: front	3.50 x 18
rear	4.00 x 18

WEIGHT

Curb weight	440 lbs.

PERFORMANCE

Maximum output	42 bhp at 7,000 rpm
Maximum torque	N. A.
Maximum speed	109 mph
Acceleration (0 to 60)	7.3 sec.

ENGINE

Type	4-stroke
Displacement	593cc
Bore x stroke	72mm x 73mm
Cylinders	Two, opposed
Compression ratio	9.5:1
Starter	Kick lever

FUEL SYSTEM

Carburetors (2)	Bing, 1/26
Fuel tank capacity	4.5 gal.

LUBRICATION

Engine	Pressure, wet sump
Oil capacity	4.25 pts.
Gearbox	1.7 pts.

IGNITION SYSTEM

Ignition	Magneto
Ignition timing	9° BTC
Spark plugs	Bosch W 260 T1

ELECTRICAL EQUIPMENT

Generator	Shunt type
Battery	6 V, 16 AH
Headlight	6 V, 35W/35W
Tail/brake lamp	6 V, 5W/18W
Turn signal lamps	6 V, 18W
Neutral indicator lamp	6 V, 2W
Speedometer lamp	6 V, 0.6W
High beam indicator lamp	12 V, 2W
Turn signal indicator lamp	6 V, 2W

(continued)

15

SPECIFICATIONS, MODEL R 69 US (continued)

TRANSMISSION SYSTEM

Clutch	Dry, single plate with diaphragm spring
Transmission gears	4-speed, constant mesh
Gear shifting	Left foot, lever-operated, return change
Final reduction ratio	3.375:1

Transmission gear ratios

1st	4.171:1
2nd	2.725:1
3rd	1.938:1
4th	1.54:1

Overall reduction ratio

1st	14.08:1
2nd	9.20:1
3rd	6.54:1
4th	5.20:1

SUSPENSION

Front suspension	Hydraulically dampened leading-link fork
Rear suspension	Swing arm with hydraulically dampened three-way adjustable units

BRAKES

Front brake	Internal expanding, double-leading shoe
Rear brake	Internal expanding, single-leading shoe

INDEX

16